CHILDREN OF THE GILDED GHETTO

Children of the Gilded Ghetto

CONFLICT RESOLUTIONS OF THREE
GENERATIONS OF AMERICAN JEWS

by JUDITH R. KRAMER

and SEYMOUR LEVENTMAN

ARCHON BOOKS
1969

SBN: 208 00842 X
Library of Congress Catalog Card Number: 78-92578
Printed in the United States of America

Contents

v

Tables

Foreword

FREE OF OPPRESSION in the new world, Jews have reaped the rewards of an open-class society, surviving both push-carts and prosperity. They enjoy the fulfillment of the American dream in "separate, but equal" communities that endure in spite of all sociological predictions to the contrary. Although the continued vitality of the minority community remains a source of sociological wonder, we propose neither to elaborate the hardships of Jewish existence nor to engage in the ancient polemics of survival. Our intent is rather a systematic analysis of the social structure of the minority community because it is the community that serves as back-drop for the drama of the changing generations.

Sociologists have long been concerned with the method-ology of understanding the many ways in which the social structure affects individual lives. Their scientific faculties are perennially challenged by both the richness of reality and the richness of theory; to do justice to both taxes their methodological ingenuity to its utmost. Somehow the social facts and fancies contributed to the empirical substance of the discipline by those subject to sociological scrutiny must be incorporated into a theoretical frame of reference. There are, however, no well codified rules to guide the investigator in his intent to relate social reality to sociological theory.

Floundering in a maze of data, sociologists frequently find themselves at a loss to explain the nature of a particular social structure and look to their respondents to supply the necessary concepts. The sociologist who falls prey to the temptation to abdicate his theoretical responsibilities to his subjects can never know more than they do; the price of his intellectual ease is a view of society limited to the perception of informants little aware of the structural forces impinging upon their daily lives. What passes for theoretical explanation in many studies may thus be little more than a sociological translation of the ideological perspectives of selected individuals unable to see beyond their own positions in the social structure.

It is one thing to learn from the mishaps of others and quite another to know how to avoid them. Fortunately, the sociological tradition of community study is one that offers resolutions to its own difficulties. Wary of the consequences of confusing data with theory, we undertook our study with a theoretical frame of reference that was constructed independently of the empirical findings; the sociological issues were defined in terms of the theory rather than the data. The methods of data collection and analysis, although by no means unique in the area of community study, were designed to answer specific questions raised by the theoretical formulation of the problem. The calculated interplay between theory and method made possible an explanation of the changing structure of the minority community that transcends its members' ideology-bound understanding of their own social patterns; respondents were asked to provide data to test theoretically derived hypotheses rather than to furnish *ad hoc* explanations of unanticipated relationships. If there is any justification for a methodological introduction to a study that claims no new methodological contribution, it is to highlight the relevance of the theory, method, and data for understanding the relationship between social structure and individual lives.

Theoretical statements that are not formulated after the fact are sometimes introduced early in the presentation of a research report only to be ignored in the interpretation of the data. An historical understanding of the social situation under survey not only adds depth to the analysis of the data; it helps to keep the theoretical conceptualization within the bounds of reality.

The conflict resolutions of theoretical interest to us, for example, are as much a product of the past as of the present structure of the Jewish community. We therefore initiated our study with a survey of the relevant historical materials on the three generations of Jews in America. This review suggested the ways in which the social situation of each generation has changed. Systematic interpretation of the historical findings in terms of our theoretical framework provided the basis for predicting the stratification of life chances in the second generation and the changes expected in the third generation.

The Jewish community of North City—a Midwestern American city—was selected for study because it was both accessible and reasonably representative of the minority situation of American Jews. The particular social setting of any community imposes certain limitations on a sample drawn from it, and consequently on any data obtained from the sample. Knowledge of the historical circumstances that have shaped a given community, however, protects the investigator from the pitfalls of undue simplification and unwarranted generalization. An understanding of both past and present social conditions permits a more valid formulation of research instruments and a more meaningful interpretation of the findings. Historical data on the community were gleaned from the recorded histories of North City and its Jewish community, previous surveys conducted by local government and social agencies, newspapers and periodicals, and the accounts of such informants as rabbis, defense agency leaders, and social workers in a position to have an inside view of community affairs.

The history of the community suggests the restrictive effects of local anti-Semitism and the pressures for in-group participation generated by the exclusive practices of the larger community. It is a community with a high degree of institutional affiliation; any sample of Jews from North City, regardless of class and status, is characterized by more participation in Jewish organizations than is likely to be found elsewhere. Another characteristic of a North City sample is the underrepresentation of Jewish organization men because of the discriminatory employment policies of local industries. There are fewer Jews in nonprofessional salaried occupations in North City than in the East.

The samples for the study were composed of one hundred respondents from each generation. Our focus on the structure of the minority community led us to select males as respondents since the determinants of class and status operate more directly in the social roles of men. The second-generation sample was randomly selected from the membership lists of two clubs representing high and low status in the Jewish community. Third-generation respondents were drawn (with the help of informants) from the ranks of the clubs, organizations, and synagogues known to recruit younger members of the community. Systematic effort was made to include in the third-generation sample all those not affiliated with Jewish organizations who could be located through their informal participation in Jewish social circles. Although these procedures introduce some bias in the direction of organizational affiliation, the resulting sample is representative of Jews in North City, if not of the United States. We are dealing with the social structure of a highly organized community and it is, after all, the affiliated Jews who constitute the community.

The new occupations of the third generation in North City are represented by the salaried professions rather than by executive positions in industry. Although these occupa-

tions provide adequate data for assessing the changing stratification of life chances among young Jews, they introduce
a problem in analysis. Many of the salaried professionals are
not natives of North City so that the social consequences
of the third generation's occupational redistribution may be
affected by geographical differences. The eastern-born symphony musicians, university faculty, research scientists, and
technical experts now living in North City are nevertheless
representative of geographically mobile young Jews who
settle in whatever community offers the most promising
professional opportunities.

The research was designed to establish theoretically determined relationships among class, status, and generation variables rather than to measure the frequency with which a
particular response occurs in a given population. The
samples were thus selected to test specific hypotheses about
the resolutions of conflict in a minority community rather
than to permit generalization about all American Jews. To
ascertain the relative proportions of response in a given
generation requires a sample rigorously representative of
that generation. To explore the sociological consequences
of particular variables, however, requires a sample selected
in terms of these variables (i.e., high and low status, second
and third generation) that is sufficiently large and heterogeneous to include the variety of responses occurring in the
population.

Interview schedules, pretested in pilot investigations, were
used in both phases of the study as the research instrument
most suited to eliciting information about in-group behavior
and attitudes. Both high- and low-status Jews and second-
and third-generation Jews were compared in terms of their
economic, social, and religious characteristics and the significance of the difference between them tested by the appropriate statistical techniques. The interview provided the
necessary data on such economic variables as occupation,

income, education; on such religious variables as synagogue membership and attendance and religious observance; and such social variables as neighborhood, friendship patterns, and organizational membership. (Third-generation respondents were able to provide such data about their fathers as well as themselves.) Included in the interview schedule for the third generation were open-ended questions about the perceived consequences of Jewish identity in order to uncover the tensions created by its minority situation most salient to the younger generation; the responses to these questions provided insights that proved useful in interpreting the statistical findings.

Although a systematic set of theoretical propositions will direct the sociologist's attention to the significant relationships to be found in his data, such propositions do not guarantee an understanding of the subtleties of meaning that inhere in any array of social facts. Insight into the patterns of behavior and attitudes that characterize the members of a particular community may derive from two sources: participant observation in the community to provide a more intimate knowledge of the social context in which behavior and attitudes occur and sympathetic rapport with respondents to elicit the insider's point of view. The sociologist cannot afford to stand too far from the sources of his data; he maintains his distance at the risk of sacrificing *verstehen*, or an understanding of the meaning of social patterns for those who live by them. (It is when he is without such understanding that he is most likely to demand that his informants come equipped with their own sociological explanations.)

We gathered as much information as possible about the informal structure of North City's Jewish community from a variety of sources, doing our best to keep abreast of its daily affairs. Student life, however, left little time (or inclination) for further involvement in the community. While our detachment from the community served to assure respondents of the anonymous and confidential nature of the interview, our membership in the minority group led to a freer expression of in-group sentiments than is usually characteristic of sociological surveys. So important was a shared universe of discourse to many informants that they demanded assurance of the interviewers' Jewish background before volunteering certain responses (especially those reflecting their less public attitudes about the dominant group). We are certainly not the first to find that in survey research, interviewer "neutrality" for its own sake is less valuable than the kind of rapport that makes it possible to obtain the desired data. The reward for eschewing a spurious detachment is a wealth of detail about the minority situation from those who experience it.

It is with pleasure that we acknowledge those who helped us to realize our sociological intentions. We share equal responsibility for the published product, which represents the combination of two independent studies; the stratification of the second-generation community was investigated by Seymour Leventman and its transformation with the third generation by Judith R. Kramer.

Community studies require, above all, the cooperation of the community; this we received in abundance. We are grateful to our informants for taking time from their busy schedules to further the cause of social research. We extend special thanks to Monroe Schlactus, regional director of the Anti-Defamation League, who so generously put at our disposal the fruits of his long experience in the community, providing both facilities for mimeographing and perceptive insights into Jewish communal life.

The reader will certainly share our appreciation of Professor John Sirjamaki, Elaine Wollan Mates, and Thelma Shoher Baker for their careful reading of the manuscript in its earlier versions. Their critical faculties served as an impetus for a more literate sociological product. Acknowledgement is made of the assistance of Bernice J. Kramer in the proofreading stage of the manuscript. The editorial assistance of Marian Neal Ash and Anne Firth Murray of the Yale University Press is also gratefully acknowledged.

Our intellectual debt to Professor Don Martindale, who spurred with the sting of the gadfly and comforted with the salve of the mentor, is one we are proud to have incurred. We will only begin to fulfill our obligation to him as we pass on the sociological tradition to others.

JUDITH R. KRAMER
Brooklyn College

SEYMOUR LEVENTMAN
University of Pennsylvania

February, 1961

Part One

LIFE CHANCES
AMONG THREE GENERATIONS OF JEWS

1
The Changing Generations

THE MINORITY COMMUNITY, however chosen its people, enjoys no special immunity to social differentiation. The ideological commitment of its members may nevertheless obscure the cleavages that exist within the community. Because minority-group members are all in some way subject to exclusion from full participation in the dominant society, they frequently claim for themselves the equality of a shared destiny. Out of deference to its underprivileged plight, observers too often portray the minority community as a homogeneous social entity whose members form a peerage founded on similarly fixed positions in the larger society. Differences do exist among minority-group members, however, and these differences influence their relative access to social values.

As members of a minority group, individuals do, of course, share a common life situation, but the situation is itself differentiated by the structure of the minority community. Like all communities, the minority community is differentiated by the sociological principles of stratification and generation. There are, for example, rich Jews and poor Jews, young Jews and old Jews. That it makes a difference to be rich or poor, young or old goes without saying; what particular difference it makes in the Jewish community piques our sociological curiosity.

Life chances are distributed in terms of generation and

3

stratification in all communities, affording some individuals greater access than others to critical social values. The minority-group situation, however, is complicated by competing sets of values: those of the minority community and those of the dominant society. To understand the structure of the contemporary Jewish community and the values on which it rests requires some consideration of the changes that have taken place over time. Because Jews are members of a minority group, their life situation is usually viewed as a response to exclusion by the majority group. The minority group, however, is not the result of external forces alone; it is also the historical product of preceding generations. Each generation represents a new response to the stratification of life chances in the community.

The Jewish community, like all minority communities, has been transformed in response to the changing social tensions of the minority situation. The variations in patterns of behavior that underlie the structure of the Jewish community, however, cannot be accounted for solely by shared minority tensions. Even the briefest review of the past reveals differences in behavior reflecting differences in life chances produced by generation and stratification. A sociological sketch of three generations of American Jewry illustrates the ways in which age and social position influence the response to the minority situation.

Each generation faces a new set of social tensions, and "every generation revolts against its parents' way of being Jews."[1] The changing conflict resolutions of succeeding generations provide the dynamics of the minority social structure, linking individual responses to institutional patterns. The resolutions of one generation, the "parents' way of being Jews," become the problem situation requiring

1. Anonymous, "An Analysis of the Jewish Culture," in *Jews in a Gentile World*, Isacque Graeber and Stuart Britt, eds. (New York, Macmillan, 1942), p. 253.

resolution by the next generation. With each generation, there is an increasing incorporation of non-Jewish values into its resolutions, which transform the structure of the minority community. The further removed the generation is from its immigrant forebears, the greater the access to the values of the dominant society. Within each generation, high status is accompanied by increased participation in the general community. How have these patterns become established? [2]

Between 1881 and 1914 some two million Jews fled Eastern Europe seeking relief from poverty and persecution.[3] Long resigned to exile, they sought only a way to stay alive. These fugitives from the Pale of Settlement [4] did not delude themselves with hopes of returning to the old country. They brought with them their women and children and prepared to settle in still another alien land.

Immigration left no sphere of life untouched by the tensions of change and conflict, but the most immediate problem was that of economic survival. With few skills and less capital, they had to eke out a living in a rapidly

2. A study of the changing structure of the American Jewish community is really a study of Eastern Europeans and their descendants. Their influence overshadows that of the earlier German arrivals, who failed to form separate communities and thus set no precedent for the future. As the last and most numerous Jewish migration to the United States, Eastern Europeans now constitute the dominant strain in the Jewish community, and it is their patterns of response that prevail. Social class, rather than national origin, provides the major source of variation in the contemporary community.

3. Nathan Glazer, *American Judaism* (Chicago, University of Chicago Press, 1957), p. 62.

4. The Pale of Settlement, imposed by the czarist regime, designated those areas of Russia and Poland in which Jews were allowed to live. Forcibly confined to ghettos, Jews endured the deprivations of economic and educational restrictions only to suffer the violence of pogroms.

industrializing society. Most of the immigrants survived
in ways already familiar to them in Eastern Europe. Some
took up the peddler's pack, others the tailor's needle, entering the lowest levels of the garment industry.[5]

These occupations offered more than the lure of familiarity. Peddlers worked for themselves and tailors for other
Jews; either condition of employment permitted the immigrant to continue in the path of orthodox piety. The
hazards of the sweatshop were many, but it offered one of
the few means of economic survival available to the Eastern European immigrants. While death and mobility took
their toll, the steady influx of new arrivals replenished the
ranks of the garment workers, who labored always in the
hope of a better future for their children.

The prospect of economic survival without social survival offered little comfort to a generation for whom religion was as vital a concern as life itself. The immigrants
wanted to live, but they wanted to live as Jews. They
sought out their *landsmann* in the corners of the cities
where they huddled and recreated the familiar ghettos of
the past in the urban slums of the new world.[6] Here was
the only security the first generation knew, a security
founded on the traditional way of life memorably engraved
in the annals of social science by Louis Wirth.[7]

5. In 1900, 60 per cent of the Russian Jews in the United States
were workers in the garment industry and 15 per cent were in
trade. Nathan Glazer, "Social Characteristics of American Jews,
1654–1954," *American Jewish Yearbook, 56* (Philadelphia, The
Jewish Publication Society of America, 1955), 11 and 12.

6. In 1920, 88.6 per cent of the immigrants of Russian origin
(most of whom, during this period, were Jewish) lived in urban
areas (in contrast to little more than one-half of the total white
population), particularly the large cities of the East. E. P. Hutchinson, *Immigrants and Their Children, 1850–1950*, Census Monograph
Series (New York, John Wiley, 1956), pp. 24, 26.

7. Louis Wirth, *The Ghetto* (Chicago, University of Chicago
Press, Phoenix Books, 1956).

The institutions of the ghetto provided time-proven means of preserving the separate identity of Jews. Patterns of behavior carried over from Eastern Europe, where Jews had lived with little contact with surrounding cultures, continued to protect the first generation from the debilitating secular influences of the dominant society. America was strange, but the minority situation was not, and these immigrants had brought with them the techniques of social survival.[8]

The ghetto was a complete, albeit narrow, social world organized around traditional religious values that permeated even the smallest detail of existence. It was, above all, a ritualistically correct community with the synagogue at its core. Religious orthodoxy constituted a way of life for immigrants aware of few alternatives. The more peripheral and less specifically religious institutions contributed to the communal solidarity that supported conformity to the demands of piety.

There were, of course, variations in response to the tensions of social survival. Some immigrants had been susceptible to the forces of secularization in Europe; even more succumbed in the new world. Religious ritual was a luxury not everyone could afford. When there came a choice between work and prayer, not a few of the 613 commandments gave way to economic necessity (particularly among young immigrants). Still, the first generation, circumscribed by the social boundaries and traditional values of the ghetto, did its best to preserve its religious heritage.

There was little opportunity for class distinctions to

8. The ghetto emerged as a result (perhaps unintended) of traditional patterns of behavior rather than of purposive action. The function of these patterns, however, was to perpetuate a religious tradition that required a communal existence. Social isolation was the result, rather than the intent, of the immigrants' desire to survive as Jews.

emerge in a generation struggling merely to survive.[9] Those
social differences that did exist in the ghetto were based
on time of arrival and degree of Americanization. These
differences had little influence on the distribution of life
chances in the first generation. Committed to traditional
Jewish values, the immigrants, however secularized, worked
out their social destiny within the confines of the ghetto.
Isolation from the world of non-Jews protected them both
from knowledge of alternatives and from conflict straining
the bonds of communal sentiment.

The ghetto changed little as long as there were immigrants to people it. Mass immigration came to an end with
the Johnson Acts of 1921 and 1924, and the structure of
the Jewish community began to change with no little prod-
ding from the children of the immigrants, whose voices
were heard in the ghetto heralding a new era.[10]

If the tensions of the first generation were those of survival, the tensions of the second generation were those of
success. The immigrants lived to tell their tale, but left it
to their children to make the social advances. The latter
wished not merely to survive in an alien land, but to better
themselves and become "real Americans" (goals which
were virtually synonymous to this generation). As members of the second generation began to strive for the values
of the dominant society, they introduced the seeds of conflict into the minority community.

9. More social mobility appears to have occurred among immigrants settled in the Midwest, where they were more likely to
be self-employed. Starting as peddlers, some eventually became merchants or small manufacturers. See Jessie Bernard's "Bi-culturality:
A Study in Social Schizophrenia," in *Jews in a Gentile World*,
Graeber and Britt, eds., pp. 264–93, for an analysis of a Midwestern
Jewish community.

10. By 1920, the immigrants were outnumbered by their native-
born children, who were coming into their maturity in the decades

The younger generation formed the ghetto's most important link with the world outside, but its contact with America had kindled the desire for the social rewards afforded by acceptance in the general community. The adolescents of the second generation tried to educate their parents in the ways of American life, but encountered the resistance of those anxious to stem the tide of secularization. Mediating between two mutually exclusive ways of life produced conflicts whose inevitability only heightened the tensions experienced by this generation.[11] The second generation's passion for all things American led finally to the rejection of the traditional values of the ghetto.

The conflict between the generations reached its peak over religious issues. The orthodoxy of the immigrants, which embodied the very cultural differences their children wanted to eliminate, isolated them from the mainstream of American life. As such, it impeded the prospects of social mobility. The second generation rebelled against its parents as the agents of a way of life long institutionalized in religious practices that now stood in the way of success, American style. The distinction between personal and cultural conflict frequently became blurred in the heat of battle, but nothing less than the traditional values of the ghetto were at stake.

Caught between the ghetto and the larger society, members of the second generation suffered the common fate of marginality.[12] They fled the ghettos of their childhood

after the first world war and asserting themselves in the Jewish community. Hutchinson, *Immigrants and Their Children*, pp. 13–15.

11. See Oscar Handlin, *The Uprooted* (Boston, Little, Brown, 1951) for a poignant analysis of the tensions between immigrants and their children.

12. Culture conflict and marginality are not inherent in the second generation, but occur in whatever generation experiences meaningful contact with the dominant culture. In isolation from

only to find themselves rejected by the general community. They wanted to live as individuals free of the onus of a special social identity, but they were still regarded as Jews, unqualified to participate as equals in the dominant society.

The community of the second generation emerged as a resolution to this social dilemma; it was sufficiently acculturated to suit its Jewish residents and sufficiently segregated to suit the members of the majority group. This was an ethnic community, predominantly Jewish, but adapted to a middle-class American style of life with institutions peculiarly suited to meet its requirements.

Economic mobility paved the way out of the ghetto; increasing concentration in middle-class occupations laid the foundation for the ethnic community of the second generation. Although not all members of this generation advanced equally, available studies suggest that most of them did advance beyond the occupational level of their fathers to achieve middle-class status more widely and more rapidly than other ethnic groups. Their mobility occurred particularly in trade and commerce, and almost as strikingly in the independent professions.[13]

The marginal position of second-generation Jews in the American economy yielded them more visibility than power, but allowed them the self-employment they wanted.

---

the general society, an ethnic subculture (such as that of the rural Scandinavian settlements in the upper Midwest) can maintain its traditions for several generations without economic or social penalty. Jews, predominantly urban, underwent the process of acculturation at an accelerated pace.

13. For evidence of the occupational mobility of the second generation see Nathan Goldberg, "Occupational Patterns of American Jews," *The Jewish Review, 3,* No. 4 (Jan.–Mar. 1946), pp. 262–90; William Kephart, "What is Known About the Occupations of Jews" in *Race Prejudice and Discrimination,* Arnold Rose, ed. (New York, Knopf, 1951), pp. 131–46; Glazer, "Social Characteristics," pp. 20–4.

They worked hard, motivated perhaps, as Kurt Lewin suggests, by their very marginality,[14] to achieve the success that provided an escape from the world of their fathers. Although the occupations of the second generation offered a minimum of prestige and a maximum of risk, they afforded the necessary income for a new style of life.

The second-generation community, located in the better neighborhoods of the city, emulated the structure of the general community with a multitude of institutions parallel to those of the larger society. Yet it retained its fundamentally ethnic character. It was, in effect, a gilded ghetto whose social life was carried on exclusively with Jews of appropriate status. The institutions were all middle-class, but the participants were all Jewish. The social distance between the minority community and the general community had yet to be bridged. As a result of both exclusion and exclusiveness, second-generation Jews were well insulated from any but impersonal economic relations with non-Jews. The gilded ghetto thus furnished the prerequisite of social segregation essential for conformity to its special values.

In the exodus from the ghettos of their fathers, the sons left behind the traditions of religious orthodoxy that might have slowed their flight. Few, however, rejected their Jewish identity. In their maturity, religious rebellion was replaced by a search for religious forms capable of perpetuating their identity. Orthodoxy wouldn't do; they had acquired a middle-class inclination to make distinctions between the sacred and the secular unknown in the ghetto, where all of life came under the aegis of the sacred. What the second generation required were religious institutions adapted to the norms of its new status.

The religious resolution of the second generation, the

14. Kurt Lewin, "Psycho-Sociological Problems of a Minority Group," *Character and Personality*, 3 (Mar. 1935), 178–85.

Conservative synagogue,[15] restructured traditional patterns in accord with those of the majority group, reducing the scope and significance of religion until it became just another specialized institution. Once a place of both worship and study, the synagogue was now assigned a single task: to inculcate the third generation with a Jewish identity. This perpetuation of the religious identity was intended to guarantee the social continuity of the minority community.

The ethnic community, whose survival could be endangered by the changing aspirations of a new generation, was a community clearly differentiated along economic lines. Class distinctions among second-generation Jews significantly affected the distribution of life chances; higher-status Jews gained greater access to the values of the dominant society than lower-status Jews. Interestingly enough, achievement of majority values reinforced the social foundations of the ethnic community. During the transition from ghetto to gilded ghetto, the second-generation community had more ecological than sociological reality. Jews associated with each other, but they were too busy establishing themselves to establish a community. The impetus for a more organized social structure came from the economic advances of successful Jews eager for a social matrix in which to enjoy the fruits of their labors.

Excluded from the general community, businessmen and professionals, supported by Jewish patronage, were susceptible to the attractions of an ethnic community. Their communal sentiments were readily converted into social reality by the professional community organizers among

15. See Marshall Sklare, *Conservative Judaism: An American Religious Movement* (Glencoe, Ill., Free Press, 1955) for a sociological analysis of the Conservative synagogue. An illuminating case history of the emergence of such a synagogue can be found in W. Lloyd Warner and Leo Srole, *The Social Systems of American Ethnic Groups* (New Haven, Yale University Press, 1945).

Jewish social workers and fund-raisers. Traditional welfare activities became the basis of formalized secular organizations, reaffirming sentiments of mutual identity and strengthening communal bonds. The now overorganized structure of the second-generation community has continued to impose communal ties and sentiments on its members, which in turn support the structure. It is no longer possible to determine whether the structure is a consequence of the sentiment or the sentiment a consequence of the structure.

Isolation from social contact with non-Jews encouraged the second generation to seek its status audience among Jews. Deprived of social recognition in the wider society, members of this generation legitimized the status they achieved within the bounds of the minority community. Like others who have gained economic, but not social, status, they responded by emulating the style of life of non-Jewish society, developing a complex system of parallel institutions within the separate but equal ethnic community. Although they adopted the symbols of middle-class life, their social isolation encouraged an appreciation of the rewards of in-group sociability.

Invidious distinctions among second-generation Jews, concentrated in a narrow range of occupations, have rested on material accumulation. Lacking occupational variety and economic *yichus* (the prestige of old and respected family businesses), this generation substituted money as the measure of success. Money, and what it can buy, has remained the major source of status stratifying the gilded ghetto and justifying its popular appellation. The economic differentiation of the ethnic community has had consequences for all its institutions. Variations in religious patterns, for example, continue to reflect the requirements of different social strata; the Orthodox, Conservative, and Reform synagogues are still associated with lower-, middle-, and upper-class Jews respectively. Similar social cleavages are found in the clubs and organizations of the second generation.

Like the generations preceding it, the third generation responds to the only world it knows, the world of *its* fathers. The children of the immigrants fled from the ghettos, rejecting in their entirety the resolutions of the first generation. They lived as marginal men in their own middle-class communities. Their children, however, are no longer caught between two mutually exclusive worlds. The life chances available to the third generation demand neither total rejection nor total acceptance. Its life situation is a highly differentiated one calling for selective and varied responses. Although there is little systematic sociological knowledge of the third generation, impressions and judgments abound. Even random observation of the younger generation suggests that it can respond to the resolutions of its fathers by (1) accepting some unchanged, (2) accepting others with modification, and (3) rejecting still others.

Secure in their middle-class American background, members of the third generation can afford to be discriminating about their fathers' resolutions. They feel no urgency to escape the world of their fathers. Some aspects of this world are quite acceptable, others require little adaptation to become so. Whatever little has been rejected has as yet escaped the notice of sociologists.

The third generation appears disinclined to reject resolutions in the areas in which its fathers had been most rebellious. Members of this generation are not so eager to avoid the occupations of their fathers as their fathers were before them. The first generation had little to pass on to its sons but the sweatshops of the garment industry, an inheritance the sons were reluctant to accept. Instead, members of the second generation established themselves as businessmen and professionals, an occupational heritage their sons find little reason to despise.

The more successful of the economic resolutions of the second generation are readily accepted by the third. This is one aspect of its fathers' world it can ill afford to disdain. Here and there a young man spurns the family business, and there are still those whose fathers have nothing to bequeath them. By and large, however, the economic tractability of the third generation has led some observers to accuse it of being wanting in the motivation necessary for achievement. Not without reason does this generation lack its fathers' drive for mobility. Its choice of occupation is neither a result of economic necessity nor an escape from a despised way of life. As college graduates, third-generation Jews can choose careers in the same fields attracting non-Jews, impelled by similar desires for security and status.

Those for whom a profitable family business awaits rarely object, but those who are not so endowed find employment in occupations outside the limited range of alternatives from which the second generation had to choose. Less concerned with success than security, those who do not have the assurance of inherited work seek their security in the occupations of organization men, characteristically considered non-Jewish occupations (the salaried professions, for example).[16] These occupations, new for Jews, attract the third generation with the lure of higher status in the dominant society (although not necessarily more income) than that afforded by more traditional sources of livelihood.

This occupational redistribution paves the way for par-

16. Recent occupational statistics reveal an increase in salaried employment among Jews, particularly striking in such professions as engineering, architecture, journalism, and college teaching. See Glazer, "Social Characteristics," pp. 26–7 and Nathan Goldberg, *Occupational Patterns of American Jewry* (New York, Jewish Theological Seminary Press, 1947), pp. 42–3.

ticipation in the general community by young Jews happy
to be free of the marginal retail trades of their fathers.
Offering an escape from any ethnic uniqueness fostered
by traditional economic specialization, the new occupations
have important consequences for the life chances of the
third generation. Not only do they ease young Jews out
of the minority community; they introduce a new source
of status. Income alone no longer serves to distinguish one
Jew from another. In the third generation, stratification
is also based on occupational prestige.

The third generation's acceptance of its fathers' economic resolutions has thus been tempered by the introduction of occupational variety. The religious resolutions
of the second generation appear to require even less modification to be acceptable. Raised in a thoroughly acculturated Judaism, the third generation experiences little
religious conflict and has less cause for religious rebellion.[17]
In assenting to the religious resolutions of the gilded ghetto,
it takes on patterns of behavior that have already adapted
to American life and incorporated the principle of change.
It requires little effort to adapt them further. Any tensions
that occur in the religious sphere are resolved by simply
changing the religious institution, modifying its demands
to suit new styles of life.

Since members of the third generation find that they
can be both Jewish and successful (at least as much as

17. In the last decade, there has been an increase in the number
of Conservative and Reform synagogues, in synagogue attendance,
and in the number of Jewish children receiving religious instruction. (See Glazer, *American Judaism*, pp. 113, 116.) In *The Riverton
Study* (New York, American Jewish Committee Publication, May
1957), Marshall Sklare and Marc Vosk present interesting evidence
of the extent to which third-generation adolescents accept the religious patterns of their parents. Most of the adolescents accept
both the synagogue affiliation and the ritual observance of their
elders.

they want to be), they feel no need to shed a religious affiliation that does not restrict their life chances. They do, however, continue to modify their religious patterns in the direction of greater conformity to those of the dominant society. Their religious observance has been reduced to an occasional acknowledgment of synagogue and ritual. Sentiment exceeds commitment in the third generation, sufficing to assuage the conscience without isolating the Jew from the general community.

The still effective *raison d'être* of religious behavior is group survival. The third generation's religious observance, such as it is, continues to be rationalized by a desire to perpetuate Jewish identity. Only a few young intellectuals, puzzled voices in a Philistine wilderness, wonder whether the religion justifies the people or the people the religion.

The absence of conflict between young and old does not signify an absence of tensions for the third generation. Though the material and spiritual comforts of the gilded ghetto be legion, its heirs desert it in droves for the life of the suburbs. Apparently there are social resolutions of the second generation that its sons do reject, resolutions that perpetuate the social isolation of the minority group. Although the economic and religious resolutions of the second generation have tended to reduce the distance between Jew and non-Jew, the social resolutions have not. Its ethnic communities, densely populated urban areas with a large proportion of Jewish residents, remained distinctly Jewish in character.

The suburbs to which the third generation has taken flight not only have fewer inhabitants in general; they have fewer Jews in particular. Jews move to the suburbs for much the same reasons that everyone else does. The move, however, changes the social conditions of the minority situation and therefore has special implications for

Jews. In search of better housing and bigger backyards, young Jews often discover the added boon of non-Jewish neighbors.

New tensions are emerging in the status communities of a generation trying to escape social visibility by rejecting the exclusively Jewish world of its fathers. These tensions are status tensions created by closer contact with non-Jews. Rejecting uniqueness in social behavior, the third generation rejects a social life based solely on ethnic ties. The communities of this generation are not ethnic, but status communities in which there are more non-Jews than Jews. The suburban style of life can hardly be considered peculiarly Jewish and thus satisfies the cravings of a Philistine generation for social invisibility. Jewish suburbanites accept the values of their status communities, conforming in a way that renders them indistinguishable from their non-Jewish neighbors.

These new Philistines are not trying to disavow their Jewish identity so much as to avoid social differentiation as Jews. They reject the ideology of separateness that rationalized the parallel institutions of the ethnic community and maximize the value of togetherness in their suburban status communities. Almost convinced that there really are no differences between Jews and non-Jews, the third generation vigorously sets about eliminating any differences that remain to make a difference in the way it is treated socially.

Living in status communities in which they share a style of life with non-Jewish peers subjects young Jews to the social judgments of the larger society. They find they still have much to learn about the subtleties of the status game. No longer outsiders, third-generation Jews can't afford to be content with mere superficial emulation of non-Jewish patterns. They have broadened their status audience and now must acquire the refinements that invite its applause. The significant status judgments are those of the general society rather than the minority group, and all the factors that enter into these judgments now become important to the third generation.

Because the tensions of the third generation are status tensions, frequently over matters of taste, they increasingly involve the wives, who are, after all, the principal bearers of status in middle-class American life. Less rooted in tradition than her mother, the third-generation wife keeps up with the social advances of her husband, mindful of the importance of her activities for the family's social position. Increasingly emancipated from the extended family, her concern is with social rather than ritual correctness.

The status communities of the third generation thus make available non-Jewish values unknown to previous generations. The changes in the structure of the minority community from one generation to the next have been the consequence of an increasing incorporation of the values of the dominant society. Each generation has experienced conflict between Jewish and non-Jewish values and uncertainty about which community offers the most promising life chances. The conflict between the generations has characteristically been a conflict of values in which each generation has redefined the values in ways relevant to its own life situation; the resolutions of conflict have been in the direction of greater acceptance of the dominant values.

The isolating values of the ghetto collapsed under the impact of American life and the possibility of mobility in the general class structure. Those of the gilded ghetto gave way with increasing social contact with non-Jews. The conflict between the first and second generation was a conflict between the values of the traditional ghetto and the values of an acculturated ethnic community. The conflict between the second and third generation is a conflict between the values of an acculturated but separate ethnic community and the values of a general status community.

Increased access to non-Jewish values has had particularly important consequences for the stratification of the minority community. Whatever stratification existed in the ghetto was a function of traditional values. The stratification of the gilded ghetto was based on economic values and ethnic life styles, but in the suburban communities of the third generation, it is based on the status values of the wider society. A once-simple system of stratification has become increasingly differentiated by occupational distinctions and styles of life as the occupationally specialized members of the ethnic community have given way to the (Jewish) organization men of the status community.

The social tensions of the minority community have evolved from tensions of survival in the first generation and success in the second generation to tensions of status in the third generation. The tensions have changed with the broadening of the status audience to include non-Jews. Interaction between Jews and non-Jews has increased, changing over time from class to status relations. Access to non-Jewish values characteristic of high-status members of the second generation has thus become more widespread in the third generation. The overlapping consequences of generation and stratification in the minority community give the advantage to the young and to the rich, just as they do in the general community. Both the young and the rich have special claim to the values that confer high status.

2
Class and Ethnic Tensions

THE MINORITY SITUATION,[1] shaped by forces from within and without the community, creates tensions requiring some resolution. A glimpse at the Jewish community, past and present, discloses that the response of minority-group members to their situation is influenced by both their stratification and their generation. These principles of social differentiation determine the distribution of life chances,[2] thereby providing the minority community with indigenous dynamics of change. An analysis of the changing structure of the minority community thus invites considera-

1. A minority group is one whose members are denied full participation in the life of the larger society because of shared ethnic (racial, religious, or national) properties. Its situation therefore is one of deprived access to the dominant values. By virtue of its superior power, the dominant group controls the life chances of the minority, including access to certain occupations, educational opportunities, residential areas, social clubs, and marriage into the majority group. See Louis Wirth, "The Problems of Minority Groups" in *The Science of Man in the World Crisis*, Ralph Linton, ed. (New York, Columbia University Press, 1944), pp. 315–51; Joseph Roucek, "Minority-Majority Group Relations in Their Power Aspects," *Phylon*, *17*, 24–30; Robert Bierstedt, "The Sociology of Majorities," *American Sociological Review*, *13*, 700–10.

2. "Life chances" refers to the probability that the members of particular social groups will have access to critical values and life experiences. See *From Max Weber*, Hans Gerth and C. Wright Mills, trans. (New York, Oxford University Press, 1946), pp. 180–81.

tion of the class and ethnic tensions of succeeding generations.

The transformation of the Jewish community over time
is a result of the changing patterns of response to the minority situation. The tensions of minority-group membership have their source in the conflicts created by the overlapping institutional structures of the majority and minority
communities. The competing values of two ways of life
lead to uncertainties and contradictions in behavior for
the minority group which demand resolution. Membership
in a given social class and generation determines the means
available to resolve these tensions. Since the resolutions of
one generation may become the source of tension for the
next generation, a generation represents a unit of social
time in the process of change.

The sociological significance of a generation, elaborated
by Karl Mannheim,[3] lies in the fact that its members share
a common location in the social structure and in the historical dimension of the social process. Membership in a
generation, like membership in a social class, limits an
individual's range of experience and influences his pattern
of response. The conceptual value of generation in the
study of changing social structures lies not in the specification of age-graded groups, but in the illumination of
shared social experiences.

Each generation undergoes a changed relationship with
its cultural heritage that results in new social meanings
and new patterns of behavior.[4] The shared meanings and
values of a generation emerge in its encounter with a common social reality. Different generations interact with
each other, educating one another in the process. Under

3. Karl Mannheim, "The Problem of Generations," in *Essays on
the Sociology of Knowledge*, Paul Kecskemeti, trans. (London,
Routledge and Kegan Paul, 1952), pp. 290–1.
4. Ibid., p. 293.

conditions of social stability, the older generation social-
izes the younger with traditional patterns of behavior,
which continue to serve as effective means of social response. When social change occurs more rapidly, however,
the older generation grows receptive to the influence of its
juniors.[5]

In order to account for variations in behavior, Mannheim introduces a distinction between the "generation as
an actuality" and "units" within a generation. The former
exists on the basis of exposure to common experiences;
the latter form on the basis of common responses to these
experiences.

> Youth experiencing the same concrete historical
> problems may be said to be part of the same actual
> generation; while those groups within the same actual
> generation which work up the material of their com-
> mon experience in different specific ways, constitute
> separate generation units.[6]

These units create bonds between their members that may
lead to the emergence of specific groups.[7]

Mannheim was intrigued by the "non-contemporaneity
of the contemporaneous," and he found in the coexistence
of different generations experiencing the same circumstances differently a source of conflict between the generations. Not content with establishing the social milieu of
different generations, he posed a dialectic between them.
A generation is thus a unit of stratification in time, "a new
way of feeling and understanding of life, which is opposed
to the former way or at least different from it."[8]

Although few have followed Mannheim's lead, a number

5. Ibid., p. 302.
6. Ibid., p. 304.
7. Ibid., pp. 306–7.
8. François Mentré, *Les Générations Sociales* (Paris, 1920), p.

of social scientists have been interested in related problems. Most recently, Eisenstadt has attempted a functional analysis of age grades and social structure utilizing the concept of generations. His thesis in *From Generation to Generation* is that the transfer of identification from the family to the larger society is accomplished readily when the norms of the social system are in accord with those of the family, permitting the individual to attain full adult status with the behavior patterns acquired in the family. When, however, the integrative principles of the social order differ from those of the family, the individual must change his behavior patterns in order to achieve full social status. Sharing the strains of this transition, peer groups gain in importance as they offer different and wider social relations than those within the family.[9]

Eisenstadt introduces to the problem of generations a consideration of the relation between age groups and institutions. The dynamics of social change are not a simple matter of dialectical conflict between the generations. As the embodiment of principles of social organization, institutions are critically affected by the processes of change and must somehow be taken into account. Each generation responds not only to the generation preceding it, but also to the existing institutions.

Mannheim's conceptual analysis, broadened to include the relation of institutions to generations, proves useful in explaining the changing structure of a minority group. The generations, however, exist in the institutional context of a specific community which persists and changes through time. The theoretical framework therefore ac-

---

304, quoted in Rudolf Heberle, *Social Movements* (New York, Appleton-Century-Crofts, 1951), p. 119.

9. S. N. Eisenstadt, *From Generation to Generation: Age Groups and Social Structure* (Glencoe, Ill., Free Press, 1956), p. 44.

quires more empirical utility when its focus is shifted from society in general to one community in particular. A statement of the theory of generations in terms of three generations of American Jews, for example, helps to isolate the changing patterns of social action underlying the structure of the Jewish community.

If, as Mannheim suggests, a generation is an age grouping, a horizontal segment of the population whose members share certain critical common experiences and life conditions, then a theory of generations should include the following general propositions:

I. A generation experiences a common life situation with similar social tensions.
II. A generation responds to the demands of its life situation, using the means available to it, within the limits established by its common social conditions.

The following general hypothesis may be derived from the above propositions: *A generation arrives at some resolution of the shared tensions of its life situation in terms of its available means and common conditions.*

The resolution of social tensions occurs in specific institutional spheres in accordance with the prevailing social conditions and the range of available means.[10] As the conditions and means change with time, the tensions of each generation's life situation change and require new resolutions in the critical areas of social life. Characteristic pat-

10. In so far as the social conditions and available means vary within a given generation, there will be variation in the response of the generation to the tensions of its life situation. These variations are explainable in terms of the differential means and conditions and lead to the development of what Mannheim calls "generation units."

terns of behavior emerge and become normative for the members of a generation. Ideologies formulated in defense of its established values reveal the self-image of each generation.[11]

Minority-group status has largely determined the life situations of American Jews and the means available to them for resolving their shared tensions. The changes that occur in the life situation of each generation are brought about in part by the resolutions worked out by the preceding generation. The characteristic patterns of behavior of one generation become components in the social tensions experienced by the next generation, furnishing some of the means and conditions of its life situation. These new tensions require new types of resolutions in accord with the changing conditions of the minority group's position in the larger social structure and the new means available to it.

The critical experience common to the first generation was immigration. Its resolution of the tensions of survival contributed to the marginality experienced by the second generation. The response of these two generations to their minority status can be restated in terms of the propositions of the explanatory framework just presented.

    I. The first generation experienced the tensions of economic and social survival in an alien society.

    II. The first generation responded both in terms of its available occupational skills and traditional culture and in terms of the industrial and urban conditions of the American social structure.

11. The distinctive resolutions of generation units frequently occur in the realm of ideology, which has consequently been a favorite area of sociological investigation. Sociologists of Jewish life, for example, have most frequently surveyed attitudes about Jewish identity, religious beliefs and practices, and Zionism.

Derivation:

(1) The economic resolution to the tensions of survival was employment in the garment industry and retail trades.

(2) The social resolution was the establishment of a ritualistically correct community in a segregated ghetto.

(3) The religious resolution was the acceptance of orthodox Judaism. An important variation in this sphere was the acquisition of a secular ethic of self-improvement.

I. The second generation's life situation was characterized by marginality, resulting in tensions pressing for improvement of its social position.

II. Within the limits set by the restrictive conditions of the ghetto and the exclusive practices of the larger society, the second generation made use of its American education and newly acquired skills.

Derivation:

(1) The economic resolution of the tensions of self-improvement was the mobility into profitable, albeit marginal, middle-class occupations.

(2) The social resolution was the establishment of acculturated, but separate ethnic communities.

(3) The religious resolution was the adaptation of traditional religious forms to modern American life. Variations in the religious resolutions occurred in the nature of the denominational affiliation and the participation in Jewish institutions.

So complex is the web of life chances spun by a generation that membership in a generation determines the level
of access to critical social values, thus influencing the opportunity for mobility. Each generation of a minority
group must resolve the class and ethnic tensions of its disadvantaged position in the social structure. With the second
generation of Eastern European Jews, these tensions are
increasingly a function of the stratification system of the
minority community. These tensions, unique in character,
have their source in the overlapping consequences of general class [12] factors and particular ethnic factors.

Robert Park was among the first to explore the implications of class and ethnic affiliation for the minority-group
situation. It was he who pointed out that the introduction
of dominant values into the Negro subculture resulted in
the formation of classes on either side of the caste line.
"The races no longer look up and down; they look
across." [13] A more general formulation of this principle
is found in Hollingshead's statement that a social structure
may be "differentiated *vertically* along racial, ethnic and
religious lines, and each of these vertical cleavages, in turn,
is differentiated *horizontally* by a series of strata or classes
that are encompassed within it. . . ." [14]

12. Social classes are comprised of persons who share common
life chances and opportunities for obtaining economic goods and
services, which include amount and sources of income and chances
for accumulating wealth. How a person earns his living as well as
how much he earns greatly affect his chances for obtaining the
valued things and experiences of a given society. See *From Max
Weber*, p. 181 and Hans Gerth and C. Wright Mills, *Character
and Social Structure* (New York, Harcourt, Brace, 1953), p. 307.

13. Robert Park, "The Bases of Race Prejudice," *Annals*, Novem-
ber 1928, 20.

14. August B. Hollingshead, "Trends in Social Stratification,"
American Sociological Review, 17, 685.

Negroes and whites, Jews and gentiles live in separate social worlds because, as Simmel explains, an ethnic factor may "overcome all other bases of separation and amalgamate persons and interests despite their natural differentiation."[15] The ethnic world is divided by class and status values, creating a complex stratification system in which "each stratum in each vertical division is similar in its cultural characteristics to the corresponding stratum in the other divisions."[16] Rich Jews, therefore, may have more in common with rich gentiles than with poor Jews.

Class, however, does not necessarily have the same relation to status in the minority community as it does in the dominant society. Among Negroes, for example, "persons whose jobs and resources would place them in the middle class or perhaps lower middle class in the white community are at the top of the social pyramid in the Negro community."[17] This characteristic discrepancy between class and status creates special tensions for minority-group members, who find that behavior that enhances their status in the minority community diminishes their status in the general community.

The most critical consequence of these class and ethnic tensions is that members of the minority group who achieve mobility into a higher class are not accorded the status bestowed upon members of the majority group of the equivalent class. The life chances of minority-group members are restricted not only by the power of the dominant group, but also by the ambiguity of their claims to status.

15. Georg Simmel, *The Web of Group Affiliation*, Reinhard Bendix, trans. (Glencoe, Ill., Free Press, 1955), p. 160.
16. Hollingshead, "Trends," 685-6.
17. E. Franklin Frazier, "The Negro's Vested Interest in Segregation" in *Race Prejudice and Discrimination*, Arnold Rose, ed., p. 333.

The discordance in minority class and status positions is in part a function of the differential nature of the class and status hierarchies. Status rests on individual evaluations granted in an interpersonal context, whereas class is achieved independently of social acceptance in the impersonal setting of the market place. Minority-group members, therefore, make their initial and most substantial advances in the realm of class, which mitigates against the barriers erected by ethnic birth.

At the risk of remaining marginal to both communities, minority-group members must decide which social universe offers them the most promising opportunity to gain status. An instance of the difficult choice involved is related by Simmel. In Spanish Colonial America, it was the practice of Spanish officials to dispense with troublesome native leaders by granting them legal patents to join the white society.[18] The Spaniards knew that, regardless of prior communal and national loyalties, the natives valued social contact with whites. By offering legal status equality to native leaders, the colonists posed for them a deliberate dilemma between high status among their fellows and apparent peer status in the dominant society. Many rebels had too much honor at stake in their own community for the choice to be an easy one. The granting of a nominally favorable position in the dominant group has long been a technique for dealing with minority-group members who threaten the interests of the majority.[19] All the majority asks in return is the surrender of commitment to the minority cause.

The class and ethnic tensions of members of a minority group derive from the conflicting principles of organization

18. *The Sociology of Georg Simmel*, Kurt Wolff, trans. (Glencoe, Ill., Free Press, 1950), p. 281.

19. Alvin Gouldner, *Studies in Leadership* (New York, Harper, 1950), p. 190.

on which their community rests. Socially, these principles are translated into competing demands on minority-group members exerted by the overlapping stratification systems of the majority and minority communities. The dilemma of dual commitment to competing value systems is hardly unique to the minority situation. Similar life situations characterize all those who are marginal to any two communities.

In so far as a minority group is protected from marginality by social isolation, it is free of the difficulties of dual commitment. When, however, there is an ideology of equality that permits some social interaction to occur between majority and minority groups, alternative values are introduced into the minority community. Finding the values of the dominant society irresistibly attractive, minority-group members strive for them at the same time that their position in the social structure deprives them of access to its values. The desire and the deprivation combine to produce the tensions of the minority situation.

In a society in which there is no ideology justifying the birthright to a disadvantaged social position, an ethnically segregated group may hold its own social honor higher than that of the dominant group.[20] The members of such a group may then claim status in the wider society as well as in the ethnic community; their claim rests solely on economic achievement. In an equalitarian society that does not recognize the legitimacy of inherited privilege, the yardstick of material success is sufficient prerequisite for social ascent.[21] Tumin explains that rapid social mobility leads to the "creation of dual and triple hierarchies on new

20. *From Max Weber*, p. 189.
21. Seymour Lipset and Reinhard Bendix, "Ideological Equalitarianism and Social Mobility in the United States," *Transactions of the Second World Congress of Sociology*, 2 (London, International Sociological Association, 1954), 36.

class levels, thereby converting ethnic groups from culture contributing peer groups into status competing hierarchies." [22]

The acculturation of the minority group that accompanies increased contact with the larger society leads to the development of status criteria based on both traditional minority values and dominant social values. Although similar criteria stratify the majority and minority communities, each remains a distinct social entity. Members of the minority group are, therefore, confused about their status identity and uncertain about which values are worthy of aspiration.[23] Should they act as members of a particular social class or as members of a particular ethnic group? Ambiguity of status audience and commitment to competing value systems thus shape the stratification of the minority community.

The resulting class and ethnic tensions are heightened by increased interaction with the majority community. Some strata of the minority group try to resolve these tensions by striving for the values and good opinion of the dominant society. "The Jews spend millions to reform the Christians, the reform wanted is that the Christians should think better of the Jews." [24] Subject to the socially independent, yet culturally related, sets of status judgments of both the majority and the minority community, minority-group members attempt to consolidate the status criteria and resolve their tensions in various ways. For example, minority-group members may form status structures that parallel those of the dominant society.[25] Struc-

22. Melvin Tumin, "Some Unapplauded Consequences of Social Mobility in a Mass Society," *Social Forces, 36,* 36.

23. Everett Hughes and Helen Hughes, *Where Peoples Meet* (Glencoe, Ill., Free Press, 1952), p. 222.

24. Ibid., p. 101.

25. Mhyra Minnis, "Cleavages in Women's Organizations," *American Sociological Review, 18,* 48–50.

tures such as clubs and associations maintain the social distance between the majority and minority communities while providing members of both with an opportunity to enact appropriate status rituals and styles of life.[26]

Certain strata of the minority group are better able than others to meet the requirements of the general community and participate in its social life. Those less able to meet majority expectations participate to a greater extent in the traditional institutions of the ethnic community. Although members of the former strata are more sensitive to the demands of class than ethnic affiliation, their status in the minority community is high.

However varied the responses of the minority group to its class and ethnic tensions, they have in common at least the following three principles: (1) an acceptance of the legitimacy of the class and status criteria of the majority group, (2) a desire for the esteem of the majority, and (3) a widening of social participation in the majority community, particularly in those activities fostering mutual esteem.

The stratification of the minority community is linked to the differential abilities of its members to meet the social requirements of the general community. Minority-group members are stratified in terms of their comparative

26. "Life styles" refers to those material possessions (homes, automobiles, clothing, etc.) and patterns of behavior (friendship patterns, organizational memberships, etc.) which guarantee certain estimates of social honor shared by members of a given status group. Styles of life reflect the ways in which individuals spend their income and symbolize membership in particular status groups. (See *From Max Weber*, pp. 187, 300.)

The most prestigeful styles of life are often the most expensive ones, which would-be members of a given status group must be able to afford. Life style, reflecting how a person spends what he earns, is thus influenced by social class, which determines how much he earns.

access to the values of the wider society and to those of
their own community. Their behavior is, therefore, a consequence of both their minority-group status and their
class position. Tensions emerge as they experience social
closure by the minority community and lowered class and
status opportunities in the wider community. The resolution of these tensions varies with the extent of the adoption
of the values of the wider community (and the desire for
social acceptance therein) and the concomitant rejection
of the traditional values of the ethnic community (and
closure therein). This study reports the differential response of members of a particular minority group to the
class and ethnic tensions of their disadvantaged situation.

The intent of the first part of the study is to explain
differences in ways of life within the same generation of
a minority group, the second generation of Jews in the
Midwestern American city we have called North City.
Their patterns of behavior constitute the responses of
various strata to class and ethnic tensions. The hypothesis
predicts that the higher the status in the Jewish community,
the greater the acceptance of the values of the general
community and the greater the participation in it. Con-
versely, the lower the status in the Jewish community,
the less the acceptance of the values of the general community and the less the participation in it.

While membership in a given generation influences both
the conditions encountered by minority-group members
and the range of means available to resolve their class and
ethnic tensions, the specific resolutions vary with the
social stratum. Thus, generation and stratification combine
to determine the distribution of life chances in the minority
community.

Part Two

CLASS AND STATUS IN THE WORLD
OF THE SECOND GENERATION

3

The Jews of North City:
The Emergence of a Community

THE JEWISH COMMUNITY of North City is the setting for
our study. The historical and social background of the
community provides a valuable perspective for understanding the specific situation encountered by each generation of
North City Jews. The established community is a product
of the events that form its history, and the circumstances
of its emergence have influenced the contemporary social
structure. The significance of the social situation of the
sample employed in this study becomes apparent as the
development of the Jewish community is traced.

THE SOCIAL SCENE

North City, the larger setting of the Jewish community,
was first settled in the mid-nineteenth century by New
England Yankees, who took advantage of sources of water
power to build grain and saw mills. The population of North
State grew rapidly with each wave of immigration between
1850 and 1870, and shortly thereafter, North City was incorporated.

Milling and lumbering, the major industries, were controlled by the old Yankee families and their descendants.
With the building of the railroad in the 1870's, transportation became another important industry. Northern Euro-

pean immigrants who were recruited to lay the railroad
and work the iron ranges and forests soon filled the ranks
of the middle and working classes in North City. The old
Yankees and their heirs consolidated their positions of
power through strategic industrial and social alignments
and formed the upper class of the city.

The Early Migrations of Jews

The early Jewish settlers, arriving first in the 1860's from
Germany, Austria, Bavaria, Bohemia, and Hungary, performed an important function for an expanding industrial
frontier whose need for supplies was great. Many of the
westward-bound Jews of the latter decades of the nineteenth century established general and dry goods stores
in North City that served the lumberjacks, farmers, and
fur trappers who periodically came into town for pro-
visions. Among these enterprising middlemen were many
educated at leading European universities who had aban-
doned their professions in favor of the lure of business in
a period of rapid economic growth.

The German Jews were proud of their *yichus* (lineage)
and did not deny their Jewish origins. The synagogue
they soon established was a Reform synagogue, derived
from the German tradition and recreated in the American
image. Lack of specialized religious personnel, however,
made traditional observance difficult. The only other specifically Jewish organization in the city at the time was
the Montefiore Cemetery Association. The German Jews,
accepted by their non-Jewish neighbors, participated in
the civic and social clubs of the wider community, including the exclusive Thursday Night Ladies' Club. No apparent discrimination barred their integration into the
general community prior to 1880.

In 1881, the population of North City numbered approximately 50,000, of which 2,500 (5 per cent) were Jews. By 1900 the total population of the city had increased to 202,000, and the Jewish population to 8,000 (representing a decline in proportion, however, to 4 per cent). Swelling the ranks of the Jews during this period were the new immigrants from Eastern Europe. They arrived en masse, poor and untutored in secular ways, from the ghettos of Russia, Poland, Rumania, and Lithuania. They settled on the North Side of the city, a low-rent neighborhood convenient to the downtown work area. Here they followed their traditional way of life, and soon a Jewish community grew up around numerous Orthodox synagogues, Hebrew schools, and *Landsmannschaften* or *Vereins* (lodges or societies whose members came from the same country or town). Yiddish newspapers, kosher butchers, bakeries, and restaurants made their appearance. Billboards announced Yiddish lectures and theatrical performances, and the streets were crowded with Yiddish-speaking men adorned with beards and sidecurls and garbed in black frock coats and hats.

The traditional Judaism of the Eastern European immigrants was a separate way of life that isolated them from the general community. Contact with non-Jews, when it occurred, did not exceed the bounds of economic necessity; more intimate social relations were avoided. Ritual purity was sufficiently important to affect even occupational decisions. The immigrants sought work that permitted orthodox religious observance and preferred self-employment to working for a *goy*.[1] Many donned the peddler's pack or tried their hand at such marginal businesses as junk and second-hand goods. Others worked in factories, but with

1. Literally, *goy* means *nation;* the plural, *goyim*, encompasses all non-Jewish nations in much the same way as the Greek concept of "barbarians." In popular usage, *goy* refers to a gentile, or any non-Jew.

the hope of saving enough money to open a store or small business of their own. The immigrant who saved some money and had a wife who could sew bought a sewing machine and opened a "garment factory."

WHEN JEWISH PEOPLES MEET

The German Jews were shocked and embarrassed by the poverty and superstitions of the uneducated Eastern Europeans. The presence of these late arrivals, who were also Jews in the eyes of gentiles who classified all Jews as one, threatened to undermine the social position the Germans had achieved. Some, unwilling to be identified with the refugees, moved away from Jewish communal life to lose themselves in the general community as "Americans." Others formed welfare and benevolent associations to assist the Eastern Europeans. Organizations such as the Hebrew Ladies' Benevolent Society, the Jewish Loan Society, the Hebrew Home for Transients, and the Council of Jewish Women were all founded between 1890 and 1920. Wives of wealthy German Jews, under the illusion that poverty was nonexistent in North City until the arrival of the Eastern Europeans, were particularly active in the attempt to bring civilization to the "over-crowded and teeming streets of the North Side."

The Eastern Europeans were offended by the condescending matrons bearing them baskets of charity. The good ladies who collected money from their friends for needy immigrants failed to temper their charity with the special quality of sympathy, or *rachmones*, valued by the Eastern Europeans as an essential grace of giving. Nevertheless, the welfare efforts had important consequences, at least for the German Jews. Although they rejected identification with the Eastern European community, the poverty of the North Side allowed wealthy Germans to vie for status with conspicuous charity. However invidious their philanthropy, it created unanticipated ties to the Eastern European community.

The characteristic conflict between the German and Eastern European Jews stemmed from opposing views of Judaism. For the Eastern Europeans, it was an entire way of life, demanding adherence to all the traditional commandments. For the Germans, it was simply a religious affiliation that did not require a separate social existence. They valued integration into American society and warned the "backward" Eastern Europeans:

> Under present conditions, if the young people do not desert Judaism because of the harshness of their parents' religious codes which are still in keeping with what they knew in darkest Russia, it will be small wonder.

The Eastern Europeans returned the compliment by accusing the Germans of apostasy.

Eastern Europeans were not welcome in German social circles and clubs. Even B'nai B'rith, founded in New York in 1877 by German Jews, excluded them in North City. Bewildered by the Germans' rejection of Jewish communal ties, the newcomers formed their own clubs and organizations. German Jews rejected both the concept of a separate Jewish community and the specific characteristics of the emerging North Side community.

Before 1880, few Jewish organizations existed in North City, apart from occasional circles of intellectuals who met to discuss topics of general interest. Jews participated in the organizations of the general community. But the mass influx of Eastern European Jews brought with it the systematic exclusion of Jews from the social life of the larger community. By the end of World War I, the status lines between Jew and non-Jew were sharply drawn. The Athletic Club, for example, passed a resolution excluding from membership the sons of Jews who were members at the time. As their social relations with non-Jews deteriorated, German Jews reorganized their informal circles into clubs whose functions were social and whose membership was restricted to Western European Jews.

The stratification system crystallizing in the North City Jewish community of 1900 included three strata. Eastern Europeans peddling or working in factories and shops made up the lower stratum and lived on the North Side in poverty and piety. There was a middle stratum of Eastern Europeans (mostly Rumanians) who had arrived before the mass migrations and who were more comfortably established than the later immigrants. They were better educated and spoke more English than the North Side Jews. As shop owners, jobbers, and salesmen, they were able to live in middle-class neighborhoods in the city, and soon joined the Conservative synagogue.

As in most Jewish communities, the Germans were the elite. Baltzell points out, "Within the Jewish community, upper class membership was based on German ethnic origins and family position which, as in the gentile community, meant 'old wealth.' " [2] In North City, the upper stratum of educated and prosperous Western Europeans were "old settlers," an advantage based on little more than a decade or two of seniority over the Eastern Europeans. They had enjoyed success as merchants and professionals and took pride in their family lineage. They lived in better neighborhoods and belonged to the Reform Temple. Their style of life qualified them as representatives of the Jewish community in its relations with the wider community. Although they sought the social approval and acceptance of non-Jews, they increasingly associated only with each other.

2. E. Digby Baltzell, "The Development of a Jewish Upper Class in Philadelphia—1782–1940," in *The Jews*, Marshall Sklare, ed. (Glencoe, Ill., Free Press, 1958), p. 273.

A New Community

The conflicts between Western and Eastern Europeans were resolved with the emergence of a community encompassing all the socially identifiable Jews in North City. The ambivalence of the German Jews' commitment to the new Jewish community attenuated their high status in it. Leaders among the Eastern Europeans were more influential in establishing the dominant ideology of the community, setting the patterns of social segregation now traditional among North City Jews.

Ghetto existence was not entirely self-imposed. Extensive anti-Semitism impeded mobility in all areas of life, increasing the difficulties the second generation faced in escaping the ghetto. Certain real estate and residential areas were closed to Jews. In 1910, over 80 per cent of all Jews lived on the North Side. By 1945, 59 per cent still lived in the area of first settlement. The others had moved to those neighborhoods to the south and west in which Jews could purchase property; these areas soon became disproportionately Jewish. With the emergence of the Jewish community, Jews were excluded from the social and service clubs of the city. The Automobile Association of America, Rotary, Kiwanis, and other town and country clubs followed the Athletic Club's lead in adopting restrictive policies against Jews. The early decades of the twentieth century saw the systematic exclusion of Jews from participation in the community's social and civic life.

Most of the Jewish immigrants started out as peddlers or merchants; they soon discovered what limited access they had to other occupations. Economic advances were made within a particularly narrow range of occupations because of the restrictions imposed upon Jews. As late as 1947 there were disproportionately few Jewish teachers in the public schools and 30 per cent of the principals were still uncertain about or opposed to employing Jews. Jewish doctors were not accepted on all hospital staffs and had difficulty in obtaining hospital beds for their patients. No officer of the County Medical Society has ever been Jewish. In the North City Self-Survey of 1936, 60 per cent of all retail and manufacturing concerns did not hire Jews as a matter of practice. Even some Jewish firms felt they could not employ Jews because it would be bad for business. Jews have been conspicuous by their absence in all the major industries: milling, mining, and lumber. Nor have there been any Jews in banking, finance, public utilities, transportation, or insurance.

The Jewish Vocational Service of North City reports continued restrictions on the range of occupations open to Jews. The young Jewish man interested in executive employment is not likely to be placed in any of the major companies in the city. His only access to the leading industries lies in the specialized knowledge and skills acquired through advanced education. If he is interested in "business" per se, he is likely to find employment only in a Jewish firm, where he stands a reasonable chance for advancement. Because of such discrimination, many young Jews still prefer self-employment.

The exclusive practices of the larger community reinforced the subcultural pressures within the Jewish community leading to a separate social existence. Internal and external forces combined effectively to foster the development of a full range of institutions within the minority community parallel to those of the dominant society. Religious institutions were particularly important as the fundamental principle of social organization in Jewish life.

Religious institutions in the Jewish community have always been linked to its social and economic structure. The life span, for instance, of the early synagogues in North

City was as much a function of the financial status of their congregants as it was of religious fervor. The first Orthodox synagogue was established by Eastern Europeans in the 1880's and grew rapidly during the period of mass immigration. (A Reform synagogue had already been established by the Germans.) The latter part of the nineteenth century witnessed the founding of many such synagogues to accommodate the influx of new arrivals. The Orthodox synagogues of the immigrants were, and remained, characteristically lower- and working-class congregations. During the depression it was these synagogues that were hardest hit, frequently forced out of existence by bankruptcy and later reorganized by some "outsider" with the necessary funds.

The changing fortunes of Jews strengthened the relationship between their religious life and their social and economic position. The support of the old Orthodox synagogue was distributed among all members of the congregation. In time, these synagogues came to depend on their wealthier members to assume the financial burden. Eventually, however, the more successful members began to move on to congregations with higher social status. As a result, the Orthodox synagogues either had to impede the mobility of their members or lose their means of survival.

Sharing an ancient religious tradition, the immigrants recreated the spiritual climate of the ghetto in the Orthodox synagogues where they gathered to pray and to study. The synagogue was a center of both religious and scholarly activities. To perpetuate it required some means of passing on the tradition to the younger generation. In the 1890's a group of Jewish intellectuals founded an independent Hebrew school, the Talmud Torah. Located on the North Side, it provided (as it still does) daily classes in Hebrew, Jewish customs, and history for children, and served as a center of adult education and culture. At the insistence of their parents, who honored traditional learning, most second-generation Jews attended Talmud Torah. The Talmud Torah became a cornerstone of Jewish intellectual life in North City, offering special courses on the Talmud and the great Hebrew prophets and philosophers. By 1957, the Talmud Torah had over 1,100 students, the largest enrollment for a school of its kind in the United States.[3]

As some first- and, later, second-generation Jews achieved a modicum of success, they began to shed the impediments of religious piety and seek a middle road between the isolating tradition of orthodoxy and the radical revisions of Reform Judaism. The first Conservative synagogue was established in 1912. The slow breakdown of the ghetto and the disappearance of an immigrant generation no longer replenished by new arrivals foreshadowed the decline of religious orthodoxy. The second generation's rejection of traditional religious practices heralded a period of "irreligion" that persisted until World War II.

Since 1945 however, synagogue affiliation has increased greatly. (See Table 1.) All North City congregations have grown in size since the Second World War, but especially the Reform and Conservative synagogues, whose member-

TABLE 1. Number of Families Belonging to Eleven North City Synagogues in 1945 and 1957

	1945	1957
Orthodox (7)	770	900
Conservative (3)	949	1,800
Reform (1)	450	900
Total	2,169	3,600

Source: Local synagogue officials.

3. The Talmud Torah is not a parochial school. The only Jewish parochial school in North City is the Torah Academy with a present enrollment of about 75 children.

ships have doubled. Roughly 65 per cent of the city's Jews are currently affiliated with a synagogue.

These synagogues are highly acculturated institutions, retaining few of their traditional functions. Their importance in the Jewish community rests more on social than religious grounds. Services are poorly attended except on High Holidays, although the Sunday Schools have a combined enrollment of over 1,000 children. More significant than the religious activities of the synagogue are the clubs, discussion groups, and social affairs which create a milieu in which members of the congregation are able to perpetuate their Jewish identity.

Excluded from German-Jewish and non-Jewish social life, Eastern Europeans associated only with each other, forming their own clubs and organizations. As the Eastern European population grew in number between 1890 and 1920, their organizations multiplied and an increasingly complex social structure evolved within the community. One of the first clubs, established in the 1890's, was the Sons of Zion, out of which emerged two Zionist factions: the religiously orthodox and the even more fervent labor socialists. Particularly numerous were the *Landsmannschaften*, burial and benevolent societies, lodges, and *Vereins* organized during this period. In addition, many informal study and discussion groups, as well as political and reform groups, were formed.

An especially interesting organization was the Gymal Doled Club founded in 1904 by a group of Jewish college students to combat juvenile delinquency. Later, the club was taken over by businessmen who transformed it into an exclusive Jewish luncheon club. It wasn't long before the Hebrew name was deemed inappropriate for the new function of the club and changed to the Criterion Club.

Although the Eastern European immigrants were little concerned with issues of organized social exclusion, the German Jews were highly sensitive to the invidious judgments of the larger community. The Pinecrest Country Club, founded in 1921, represented the German Jews' systematic attempt to erect social barriers between themselves and the *nouveaux riches* among the Eastern Europeans. A second country club was organized several years later by some Eastern European members of the underworld who had been refused membership in Pinecrest because of their "shady reputations." Though they had to settle for an inferior golf course, the Eastern Europeans now had their own club.

With the end of mass immigration, the Jewish community passed into the hands of successful second-generation Eastern Europeans. The old Germans could neither afford the style of life of wealthy Eastern Europeans nor condone their allegedly aggressive and crassly materialistic approach to the world. Jews identifiable as German tended to disappear from the social scene; some assimilated, some moved away, and some married Eastern Europeans. German Jews who remained and maintained their separate national identity formed an unattached subculture of their own. Although the exclusive behavior of the German Jews won them distinction as snobs in the Jewish community, Eastern Europeans were not oblivious to the prestige gained from intermarriage with them. Some of the particularly eager Eastern Europeans even changed their names to German ones.

By 1957 the Jewish community in North City included over 100 organizations; the average Jew belongs to at least three. The support of these social and philanthropic activities is provided by the complexly organized fund-raising structure that developed with the growth of the Jewish community. The Federation for Jewish Social Service, created in 1930, coordinates the activities of local social service and fund-raising agencies.

The Federation, critically related to the major institutions of the Jewish community, exercises powerful social controls. For example, in order to receive financial support from the Federation, an organization must have an exclusively Jewish membership. By such means the Federation helps to perpetuate the separate existence of the Jewish community and to reinforce the social identity of its members. As a matter of fact, the operational definition of a Jew in North City, at least for purposes of local organizations, is an individual who contributes (any amount) to the Federation. During its annual spring campaign, the Federation has raised as much as $1,000,000, but contributions have been declining recently. In 1956, 5,000 people gave a total of $806,000 to the Federation, 80 per cent of which was donated by 10 per cent of the contributors.

SOCIAL ADVANCEMENT

The position of the Jewish community in North City has changed with the social advancements of its members. Advances have occurred in three major areas: residential, economic, and social.

Residential. The German Jews had originally settled near their places of business in the downtown area, but soon moved to better neighborhoods of the South Side. The Eastern European immigrants had congregated on the near North Side where most of them remained until after World War II. Economic and social mobility loosened the ties of the ghetto and led many Jews away from the area of first settlement to other sections to the south and west earlier known as "Deutschland." The upwardly mobile left the ghetto in search of nothing more impious than decent housing and respectable neighbors, appropriate symbols of their newly acquired middle-class status. Those who remained committed to the ghetto in spite of prosperity stayed on the North Side, finding middle-class housing in Green-wood. Working-class Jews still too poor to move elsewhere continued to live in the area of first settlement.

During the past two decades, the North Side has lost still more of its Jewish residents to the more attractive neighbor-hoods south and west of the city. A 1957 census of Jews in the metropolitan area found a population of approxi-mately 20,000, only 38 per cent of whom still lived on the North Side. This represents a decline of over 20 per cent in North Side residence since 1936.[4]

The fastest growing Jewish neighborhood in North City is West Parricus, a southwest suburb whose population has in-creased from 982 in 1930 to 38,200 in 1957. Twenty-eight per cent of the city's Jews now live in West Parricus, where they constitute 13 per cent of its population. The North Side is thus being supplanted as the area of greatest concentration. (About 45 per cent of the Jewish residents of West Parricus moved there from the North Side.)

The North Side has become a "tarnished" neighborhood from whose "Jewishness" the upwardly mobile flee to areas less densely populated with Jews.[5] The movement from the North Side to the suburbs represents a shift in the relative economic standing of these residential areas, as well as in their changing prestige values. The median value of one-family houses in West Parricus is $12,000, while on the North Side it is $9,500. The median family incomes of West Parricus and the North Side are $4,410 and $3,077 respec-tively. The suburb clearly represents a higher class level than the older neighborhood.

4. The number of Jews in North City has increased by 18 per cent since 1937, but their proportion in the population has de-creased from 3.5 per cent to less than 3 per cent in 1957.

5. 25 per cent of the North Side's residents are foreign-born in contrast to the 9 per cent foreign-born in West Parricus.

The depopulation of Jews on the North Side has created problems for the institutions serving the traditional Jewish community. North Side synagogues are losing their congregations at the same time funds are being raised to build new synagogues in West Parricus. To combat declining enrollment, the Talmud Torah has opened an extension in the suburbs. Membership in old North Side clubs and lodges is falling off and they face the alternatives of going out of existence or following their members to other areas of the city. Social agencies located on the North Side are struggling with loss of financial support and *raison d'être* as their donors —and clients—move away. A major overhauling of the structure of the Jewish community is imminent.

Economic and Occupational. Jewish immigrants to North City earned their livings as peddlers, junkmen, or merchants. Many eventually entered such retail and wholesale businesses as clothing, jewelry, liquor, groceries, and drugs. Some, however, were artisans who worked as independent tailors or furriers; others were employed in garment factories. Working-class Jews (of whom there are fewer in North City than in large eastern cities) tended to be skilled or semi-skilled craftsmen rather than laborers and were rarely found in heavy industry. In general, the first generation of North City Jews was concentrated in economic positions of high visibility as middlemen in trade and commerce. Their businesses,

> by their very nature, fail to invest ownership with social power and prestige. Too often these businesses lack the artisan beginning, a long identification with certain family names, and the intimate relationship to a particular community that have invested so many American businesses and the families that control them with an extraordinary social power. Clothing stores

and motion picture theaters are not nearly so impressive as mines and mills, factories and railroads.[6]

Although members of the second generation improved their economic situation, they continued to be located in the same area of the economy as their fathers. Some joined the salaried ranks of salesmen and white-collar workers, but most of them remained self-employed in the distribution of goods and services. Especially successful were those in wholesale distribution, light manufacturing, and trucking. Real estate, construction, and investments provide newer sources of income for affluent North City Jews. Like second-generation Jews elsewhere, North City Jews are also well represented in the independent professions.

The second generation unquestionably achieved economic mobility. The representation of Jews in middle-class occupations is proportionately higher than that of non-Jews in North City. A self-survey conducted in 1948 found that 31 per cent of non-Jews were employed in professional, managerial, and other white-collar positions. In contrast, 52 per cent of Jews were employed in these occupations. This mobility, however, has been circumscribed by limited access to occupational alternatives.

The continued concentration in a narrow range of occupations is apparent in the fact that second-generation Jews moving to better residential sections on the South Side have increased their incomes rather than their occupational status. There are few differences in the occupational distribution of North and South Side Jews. Wealthier proprietors and professionals moved to the south and west part of the city, while poorer ones stayed on the North Side. The defining characteristics of the neighborhoods are financial rather than occupational.

6. David Riesman, "The Sociology of Jewishness," *Public Opinion Quarterly*, Spring 1942, 41.

Social Participation. The social participation of Jews in the community has been restricted by policies of exclusion and characteristic Eastern European reluctance to associate with gentiles. Encounters between Jew and non-Jew have been limited to the impersonal meetings of the market place. This situation persisted at least as late as 1947 when a survey of 70 professional organizations, educational and discussion groups, philanthropic and welfare societies, and civic organizations in North City found that 55 per cent of them had no Jewish members.

The absence of participation in the general community is in sharp contrast to the overorganized social life found within the Jewish community. A multitude of clubs and organizations has proliferated into a complex, and frequently overlapping, social network sustained by the time, money, and energy of Jews ideologically committed to maintaining a separate social existence. Although the price may be high, the man-hours and dollars spent supporting Jewish social life buy protection from traditionally feared intimacy with gentiles.

However, the walls of the gilded ghettos have begun to crack as Jews seek association with and are accepted by gentiles. Jews have gained admittance to civic organizations, although they are still excluded from business and social clubs. "They want our money, but not our company," complain Jewish businessmen, who are invited to participate in decisions about spending money, but excluded from the inner circles where decisions about making money originate.

Friendship with gentiles (of appropriate status) is becoming increasingly acceptable to some (though not all) North City Jews. They are conscious, however, of "five o'clock shadow," or the drawing of silken curtains against further association by gentiles who are willing to meet with Jews only during business hours when social intimacy is unlikely. Upper-status Jews especially suffer social rebuff by gentiles because of their more frequent contact with them. For instance, the Symphony Ball is one of the most important social events of the year, and the dinners and receptions preceding it are always described in the social notes of the city's newspapers. Most parties given by gentiles are held at the leading (and exclusive) town and country clubs and include socially prominent non-Jews among the guests. Jewish parties include few non-Jews and are held in private homes (since the Jewish clubs are equipped only with summer facilities). The failure to publish guest lists suggests the absence of any of the social elite at the Jewish parties.

Perhaps even this social segregation is a thing of the past. In 1958, Jews participated for the first time in many of the activities supporting the Symphony Ball, including pre-ball dinners and receptions given by prominent non-Jews. Although this provides opportunity for increased social contact between high-status Jews and non-Jews, the shadow of the old "ulterior motive" lurks behind the graciousness of the unprecedented invitations. The Symphony finances are in a critical state, and every effort is being made to tap previously unexploited financial resources, including the wealth of *nouveaux riches* minority-group members. Dining and dancing with Jews once a year is one way the old Yankee patrons of the arts can maximize contributions to the Symphony and underwrite its continued existence. Whether the interests of the arts will have any effect on the social relations between Jews and non-Jews in the future remains to be seen.

IN SUMMARY: SPECIAL FEATURES OF A
NORTH CITY SAMPLE

As members of a prosperous, tightly knit, and well-organized community, North City Jews are socially bound to each other by a series of involuted relationships that rarely include gentiles. Sharing a sense of separate and collective destiny, they interact as members of an in-group whose social relations are organized around certain basic institutions. The synagogue remains a center of social life, flanked by a variety of Jewish organizations (social and philanthropic) and fund-raising activities. Reinforcing the patterns of social exclusiveness is the self-employment in trade and commerce common to most members of the Jewish community, permitting them to do much of their business with each other.

The defining characteristics of the North City Jewish community are reflected in the special features of our samples.[7] For instance, since North State did not become a state until the late 1850's, the American ancestry of North City Jews is of relatively recent vintage, rarely dating back more than 75 years. The earliest Jews in North City arrived over 200 years after the first Jews had settled in the United States, depriving them of the prestige derived from early settlement.

Members of the Jewish community in North City are predominantly second-generation Eastern Europeans; there are relatively few Western and Central Europeans and no Sephardic Jews. Religious orthodoxy and ethnic tradition are characteristically defined in terms of Eastern European norms and typically associated with the poverty and lack of secular enlightenment of the ghetto. There are no very orthodox groups such as the Hasidim.

The predominance of the mills has shaped the North City economy in a way that excludes Jews from the most important economic activities of the city. Deprived of access to any of the basic heavy industries, North City Jews are forced all the more into self-employment as middlemen. They have become the prototype of the middle class to

7. See Foreword for a discussion of the problems of sampling in the Jewish community of North City.

which working-class Northern Europeans aspire, the role models after which other immigrants pattern their upward mobility. Their claims to social honor, however, are legitimized by economic achievement in marginal businesses rather than by prestigeful ancestry or long established family businesses.

Above all, our second-generation sample particularly reflects the greater exclusion of North City Jews from the social life of the general community than exists elsewhere. The absence of interaction with non-Jews shows up in the social introversion of the Jewish community that not even the high-status members of our sample have escaped entirely.

Members of the third generation grew up highly conscious of their Jewishness during the peak of anti-Semitism in North City. Both the particular historical events of the 1930's and local social conditions combined to produce in third-generation Jews an awareness of the restraints placed upon them and of the need to "stick to their own kind." They do not forget that there are clubs they cannot join and jobs they cannot have.

Young Jews in North City enjoy fewer occupational opportunities than they do in larger eastern cities, particularly in salaried employment. Few are in typically non-Jewish occupations. Their "new" occupations are not the executive positions of organization men, but the salaried professions, which frequently demand geographic mobility of their incumbents. This mobility is a new pattern in the North City Jewish community, which, like all communities, once controlled the social fortunes of its members through loyalty to the locale rather than to the occupation. Even with some mobility out and away from the community, the social insulation from the general community remains to perpetuate strong in-group feelings.

The particular historical conditions of the North City Jewish community combine to produce a distinctive social entity, a community that is relatively new and small whose members enjoy few social and economic alternatives. Although these characteristics do indeed represent contrasts to those of the other Jewish communities in the United States, they do not detract from the striking resemblance this community bears to older and larger Jewish communities. The North City Jewish community has both special properties and properties common to the structure of all Jewish communities. The particular properties explain the special features of a North City sample; the structural properties permit generalization to other communities.[8]

RITES OF PASSAGE: SUBCULTURAL THEMES AND VARIATIONS

An uncommon, but useful clue to the nature of the social differentiation of the North City Jewish community is the way in which its members bury their dead. Two funerals,[9] occurring within months of each other, provide an introduction to the variations in style of life in the second generation that are the focus of the first part of this study.

Early in 1957, Mr. Philip J. Robbins, a wealthy and prominent member of the North City Jewish community, died. The morning paper devoted half a front page column to news of his death and the Reform synagogue in which he had been a board member held funeral services for him.

Many of his non-Jewish business associates attended the service, a dignified and unemotional one that offended the sensibilities of no one. Floral arrangements adorned the altar of the chapel and softly playing organ music created a

8. Chapter 8 includes a discussion of the generalizability of data derived from a study of the Jewish community of North City.

9. For a fascinating discussion of the funeral as a rite of passage see Arnold van Gennep, *Manuel de Folklore Française Contemporaine* (Paris, Editions Auguste Picard, 1943), Chapter 5.

hushed atmosphere. Arriving in Lincolns and Cadillacs, tastefully and expensively dressed mourners quietly entered the chapel.

The Reform rabbi appeared, hatless and without the traditional prayer shawl, attired in a simple black academic gown. He delivered the eulogy, beginning with a few lines of prayer in Hebrew, which he did not use again during the service. The rabbi portrayed Robbins as a "refined gentleman," an "integral" part of the North City community. He recounted Robbins' life as a success story of the immigrant boy who made good. The eulogy reaffirmed the value of success in this world, even with the rabbi's more spiritual conclusion, "His soul was ever-growing, Mr. Robbins died climbing." At the end of the service, the pallbearers (board members of the synagogue) carried the copper-handled, walnut casket to the hearse.

Several months later, Mr. Joseph Goldberg, a poor, religious tailor died. Funeral services were conducted in the chapel of the funeral home by the rabbi of Goldberg's Orthodox synagogue. There was neither music nor flowers in the chapel. Occasional weeping disturbed the otherwise quiet atmosphere. Only Jews were present at the funeral. The mourners, inexpensively dressed, included men who had stopped at the service during their working hours. Their attire suggested employment as craftsmen and semi-skilled workers.

The rabbi, dressed in skullcap and plain dark suit, opened the service with the traditional Hebrew prayer for the dead. He began the eulogy by stating, "We are gathered here not as individuals, but as a community to pay tribute to one of our dearest friends." The rabbi described Goldberg in terms of his personal warmth, spiritual dedication, and regular synagogue attendance. There was no mention of social or business success, but rather, "A man's riches are measured not by his bank account, but by the spiritual guidance and comfort he provides his family."

In eulogizing Goldberg, the rabbi made use of both Hebrew and Yiddish to capture the essence of his life. This was a life full of sacrifice for the children, but rewarded with *nachus* (pride and satisfaction). Goldberg had been especially proud of his children's graduation from Talmud Torah. The rabbi advised the sons that the best way to honor their father's memory was to attend synagogue frequently. At the conclusion of the service, the close friends of the deceased carried out his casket of pine.

The contrasts in the two funerals are particularly striking since both individuals are Jews and members of the same community. A Rumanian immigrant who arrived in the United States at an early age, Robbins eventually became a leading retailer of men's clothing in North City as well as a nationally recognized men's fashion expert. During his lifetime, he was a generous contributor to a variety of community causes. The eulogy, however, made no mention of Mr. Robbins' financial or personal contributions to the Jewish community, although they had in fact been considerable. Nor did it suggest his dedication to the religious and cultural values of the Jewish community.

Goldberg was also a Rumanian immigrant who arrived in the United States at an early age, but one who remained a tailor all his life. He was a long-time resident of the North Side where he was known and liked. He participated in his local community as a member of a workingmen's organization and a Community Center. His social activities, circumscribed by the confines of his immediate neighborhood, centered around the religious core of his life.

Mr. Robbins was "immortalized" for his material success, Mr. Goldberg for his nonmaterial or spiritual success. Why these differences and how to explain them?

The contrasts are in part traceable to the homes that arranged the two funerals. There are two Jewish funeral homes in North City, one of which is located on the South Side. This one handles all the funerals of the wealthy Jewish families, arranging Mr. Robbins' funeral at a cost of over $1,000. The other, located in the northern section of the city, handles most of the funerals of the orthodox and less wealthy Jews. This one arranged Mr. Goldberg's funeral, which cost less than $500. It provides the traditional type of Jewish funeral, adhering to orthodox ritual and encouraging the display of emotion during the service. This home has its own hearse and Jewish driver, while the former rents hearses, driven by gentiles. The North Side home, therefore, feels justified in advertising the "only really Jewish funeral in North City," accusing the former of being a *goyishe* home. The South Side home argues that it provides a modern Jewish funeral, observing only the rituals necessary to maintain dignity and refinement. Needless to say, North City Jews are well aware of the different types of funeral provided by each home. What factors determine whether they seek the services of one or the other?

The differences between the two funerals are in part explainable in terms of social class. For example, Robbins' funeral service was attended by a large number of wealthy business executives, whereas Goldberg's service was attended by a relatively small group of close friends and family. Robbins' service took place in a large, imposing Reform temple, Goldberg's in a small chapel of the funeral home. Robbins' funeral cost over twice as much as Goldberg's. In the words of his funeral director, Robbins was buried in a "fashionable walnut casket." In contrast, Goldberg was buried in a "plain pine box" by a family which believes in "putting people into the ground as cheaply as possible." According to the funeral director, "A family spends in death as they do in life. If a person drove a Cadillac, chances are his funeral will show it and will differ from that of a person who drove a Ford."

Important differences between the funerals, however, have no necessary relation to economic class. These differences reflect the presence of differing life styles among Jews related to the internal stratification of the community. The differences in religious character of the funerals, for example, are not to be explained simply in terms of how the deceased earned their livings or how much they earned. The amount of Yiddish spoken, the degree of emotional restraint, the presence of flowers when it had been requested that none be sent, even the front page announcement of Robbins' death cannot be so explained.

Both ethnic and class factors influence the behavior of minority-group members. The study of two strata of second-generation Jews that follows is thus an investigation of two styles of response to class and ethnic tensions.

4

Lodgniks and Clubniks:
A Study in Contrast

THE JEWISH COMMUNITY in North City encompasses a complex array of social strata, which are characterized by the distinctive values and behavior of their members. Two groups representing different class and status positions in the Jewish community were selected for study in the analysis of the stratification system. One is a country club whose members are reputed to be among the wealthiest and highest-status Jews in the community. The other is a B'nai B'rith lodge still active in the North Side area of first settlement. The social portrait of these two groups represents a study in the contrasting ways of life that coexist in the same minority community.[1]

The groups, however, do have in common the critical characteristics of their minority situation. High- and low-status Jews alike share the traditions of their subculture and the tensions of their ethnic identity. Indeed, their very membership in Jewish clubs and lodges, however disparate in status, represents a common response to the dilemmas of an acculturated, but socially insulated existence. Both the country club and the lodge are part of an intricate system of

1. The data on these two strata are based on one hundred interviews (fifty respondents, all male, randomly selected from each group).

62

organizations performing important status functions for the minority community.

Typical members of their minority group, clubniks and lodgniks are the sons of immigrants who left Eastern Europe to seek their fortunes in the United States in the decades between 1880 and 1920.[2] Their fathers were impoverished adherents of orthodoxy, unschooled in secular learning. As we have already noted, they originally settled on the North Side where most of them eked out a living as peddlers and merchants.

Caught between the Yiddish culture of the ghetto and the tantalizing prospects of American life, clubniks and lodgniks knew what it was like to be Jews, to be "different." In adjusting to the new way of life, they encountered a high degree of anti-Semitism in North City. They were members of a marginal group, forced into employment in those aspects of trade and commerce that were most risky. Although at opposite ends of the income range, both clubniks and lodgniks are still retailers, wholesale distributors, self-employed artisans, or commercial speculators.

Congregated in particular areas of the city, members of the club and lodge organize their lives around their work, striving always to prove themselves in the terms of American society. Since they are without occupational prestige, they must maximize their wealth as proof of social worth. The history of the club and the lodge is closely linked to the relative success of their members in obtaining the tangible rewards of hard work and sustained effort.

The Isaac Silverman Lodge of B'nai B'rith, founded in 1948, was named in honor of a nineteen-year-old North City Jewish boy killed in World War II. Upper-class lodges had set the precedent for naming themselves in honor of the heroic war dead (e.g., the Myron Blum Gilmore Lodge

2. Twelve per cent of the club members and 20 per cent of the lodge members were themselves born in Europe. In 1957, the average lodgnik was forty-nine years old, the clubnik fifty-one.

named for a twenty-year-old North City Jewish boy killed at Pearl Harbor), a pattern soon emulated by lower-status lodges such as Silverman. The lodge was established as a neighborhood organization to increase local Jewish activity. As one of the founders explained, "This lodge was organized by men who felt the North Side was not participating enough in Jewish affairs." There are close to 300 members; any Jew is eligible for membership.

Like most B'nai B'rith lodges, Silverman meets once a month to plan the many social activities the group engages in, one of the most popular being bowling. Bowling, however, is not the sole concern of lodge members; they also raise funds and contribute time and effort to various Jewish causes.

Pinecrest Country Club is organized along more exclusive social principles. It was formed in 1921 by a group of German Jews who resigned from the Athletic Club when it passed a resolution barring Jews from future membership. At the outset there were 85 members; currently there are over 250. The club is patterned after the typical country club popular among the *nouveaux riches* of F. Scott Fitzgerald's era, complete with golf course, swimming pool, and lavish dances and balls. The founding members were the elite of the Jewish community and almost all were of Western European descent.

The club, a symbol of hard-won success in American society, was far removed from the lives of the Eastern Europeans struggling for existence. A descendant of one of the founders justified the absence of Eastern Europeans from the early membership roster thus: "The North Side Jews didn't know what we were talking about when we mentioned golf." During the depression of the 1930's, the club was hard pressed for funds and for the first time began to solicit members at large rather than by personal invitation. By then, a new class of Jews had emerged, a class of newly rich Eastern Europeans and their sons, pursuing the pleasures of conspicuous consumption with energetic delight. Among them were both paragons of "respectability" drawn from the ranks of recently successful businessmen and such "upper shadies" as the "liquor crowd." Even ill-gotten gains, however, were useful in staving off bankruptcy, and these Eastern Europeans and their friends rapidly swelled the membership until they dominated the club.

Pinecrest membership is restricted to Jews, but open by invitation to any one of the faith willing to pay the $2,000 initiation fee and the equally costly annual dues. Since Pinecrest must remain exclusively Jewish to maintain its bond with the Federation, synagogue affiliation is required of members as evidence of Jewish identity. Pinecrest members favor the fashionable Reform Temple and its religious concessions to the social interests of high-status Jews.

The critical requirement for membership is the amount of money would-be members donate to the Federation. A receipt in evidence of contributions in keeping with income must be presented to the membership committee, appropriately made up of well-informed persons skilled in judging whether or not an individual has given as much as he can afford. The judgment of the committee on this issue is sufficient to determine the acceptance or rejection of an applicant. This policy has helped to forge the significant link that exists between Pinecrest Country Club and the Federation. The latter exploits the financial resources of the club membership in return for which the club gains greater power and prestige in the community. This mutually agreeable exchange is worked through the interlocking directorate of the Pinecrest executive board and the Federation lay board. Often the president of Pinecrest will simultaneously serve as president of the Federation board, or at least be a candidate for this position.

Money: The Root of Class Differences

In the race for economic mobility, clubniks far outran lodgniks. Concentrated in trade and commerce, club members have gained wealth as self-employed businessmen in wholesale distribution and light manufacturing. They are also the owners of chains of dry-cleaning, drug, and grocery stores. Their average annual income is $27,500, representing a range of $10,000 to $50,000. Some incomes are further implemented by investments, real estate holdings, and partial ownership of other businesses. (See Table 2.)

Table 2. Economic Class Characteristics of Pinecrest Club and Silverman Lodge

VARIABLE	Per Cent of Club	Per Cent of Lodge	Statistical Difference *
Average annual income	$27,500	$6,540	Significant
Wholesalers and manufacturers	48.0	4.0	Significant
Salvage and retail	28.0	60.0	Significant
Trade and commerce	50.0	60.0	Not significant
Self-employed	98.0	68.0	Significant
Managers and professionals	72.0	4.0	Significant
Proprietors and craftsmen	28.0	96.0	Significant

Table 3. Class-Linked Status Characteristics of Pinecrest Club and Silverman Lodge

VARIABLE	Per Cent of Club	Per Cent of Lodge	Statistical Difference *
Home ownership	96.0	90.0	Not significant
Average house value	$33,593	$13,833	Significant
Children attend private schools	22.0	0.0	Significant
Children attend private colleges	76.0	8.0	Significant
Children in professions	48.0	78.0	Significant

* These differences are based on chi-square values. See Chapter 5 for a more complete illustration and discussion of the statistical techniques employed here.

Lodgniks, on the other hand, are less well off, with incomes ranging from $3,000 to $7,500 a year, averaging $6,540.[3] Most of them are craftsmen (carpenters, plumbers, electricians) and proprietors of retail stores. The tradition of self-employment is strong among lodge members in spite of the economic difficulties and competition from big business that many of them have faced. The majority cling tenaciously to their own businesses and the shred of self-respect proprietorship offers them. One furrier, whose income during recent years has steadily diminished to a level of mere subsistence, argues that he would not consider working for someone else because, "I can't afford the risk of not knowing for sure whether I'll be paid each week." Those who are not self-employed are employed by other Jews; the source of livelihood for lodge members is thus found entirely in Jewish-owned and -controlled business.

Jewish Businessmen. Club members are self-made men who prefer active working roles in their businesses to the absentee ownership their incomes might permit. Convinced of their indispensability, they work long hours in highly individualized occupational roles, eschewing the impersonal rationality of modern business methods. Many go so far as to carry their businesses around in their heads, always ready for the affairs of the market place. They assume full responsibility for all economic decisions, fearful of delegating authority to the less knowledgeable. Even their sons and heirs, with their bachelors of business administration, must prove their worth in a trial by experience.

The businesses of the second generation are family businesses in which principles of both kinship and economy

3. The club and the lodge thus constitute an upper- and lower-class group respectively. Although they are the focus of the study, we are not unaware of the strata of middle-class Jews who make up the largest proportion of the community.

merge to produce a nepotistic system of mixed values and commitments. Since the rationale of the business lies in its contribution to the welfare of the family, the acceptance of "outsiders" is precluded. Even when nepotism gives way to rational economic organization, Jews continue to do business in a community of ethnic peers. In the wholesale and retail distribution of goods, for example, the long line of Jewish middlemen participate in economic decisions as if these decisions were a matter of mutual defense protecting a closed circle against encroachment by gentiles. Indeed, a two-price system still operates in many minority businesses, asking one price of Jews and another of non-Jews.

Many Jewish businesses are too well entrenched in the minority community to be threatened by the competition of the open market. The business world of the second generation is divided into two camps, Jewish and non-Jewish, and the interests of minority businesses are promoted by the in-group clubs and associations working in their behalf. The "enemy" is kept at bay and the success of the in-group secured.

In a period of growing oligopoly, Jewish businesses have survived in the shelter of ethnic segregation. Because Jews are excluded from the dominant business community, they are beyond the reach of its informal sanctions. They are "outsiders," marginal retail traders, who have no reason to be susceptible to the opinion of gentile colleagues who do not accept them in any case. Jewish businessmen, for example, have characteristically preferred a flexible price system to fixed prices. They have thereby performed considerable economic service as middlemen for inflation-conscious consumers and overstocked manufacturers, at the cost, however, of their social honor in the larger business community.

"Jewish businesses have no General Motors," notes one respondent, and no one to set prices. Jews have sacrificed some margin of profit for a more rapid turnover of inventory. Now considered "unfair price competition," the promotion of sales volume remains a principle of ethnic merchandising, especially in metropolitan areas. As long as Jews are socially removed from gentile business circles, they are immune to the negative judgments of the majority group, at least in the realm of economic behavior. Exploiting their marginality for their own advantage has been the one means of economic survival consistently available to Jews. One respondent recalls the "old days" when, "Give a Jew and a gentile each $1,000 to start a business, the gentile buys fixtures while the Jew buys stock, any stock. How to unload the stock, he worries about later." Low overhead and a sales force of relatives permit the smaller markup that moves the merchandise.

The businessmen of the second generation, whose interests are vested in ethnic segregation, honor the traditional values that grant legitimacy to the claims of shared birth. The cleavage between Jewish and non-Jewish businesses in North City is less a function of class divisions than ethnic exclusion and self-exclusion. Within the minority community, it is the business stratum that gives greatest credence to the value of money and the economic determination of social differences. Money has, after all, made a big difference in the lives of Jewish businessmen and its value is known even to their professional brethren.

Jewish Professionals. Independent professionals such as physicians, dentists, and lawyers constitute another stratum among the ranks of the country club. Their situation is characteristic of the position of Jewish professionals in North City. The status of Jewish physicians, for example, is tenuous. They are excluded from affiliation with leading North City hospitals and from membership on executive boards of local medical societies. One medical club member elaborated thus:

The hospitals and medical societies in the city and the state are run like social clubs, at least as far as the Jewish physicians are concerned. The inability of the Jewish physician to obtain necessary hospital affiliation and executive positions in local medical societies has seriously inhibited his economic and professional opportunities.

He further explained that lack of professional opportunities has led many talented Jewish physicians and surgeons to move to other cities to practice medicine.

The building of Mount Sinai Hospital in 1950 provided new opportunities for Jewish doctors, both for patient referrals and for medical research. It has since become one of the leading hospitals in the city. Its existence has initiated contacts between Jewish and gentile doctors to an extent never before realized by local Jewish medical men. As a result, Jewish doctors are receiving more referrals of patients from non-Jews.

In 1955, there was a fire in one of the older hospitals, seriously impeding its operation. Under such circumstances, other hospitals customarily lend what technical and professional assistance they can. When news of the fire reached them, the professional members of the Mount Sinai board were gathered by chance at a social affair. Anxious to be the first to offer a helping hand, they immediately voted to aid the stricken hospital. They acted in full awareness of the role of Mount Sinai as a *Jewish* hospital and of the possibility of enhancing its public image. There is no way of knowing whether the community interpreted their deed as that of a Jewish hospital or that of a medical Samaritan.

More promising professional prospects have encouraged Jewish doctors to specialize in fields which are "new" for them. For example, before 1950 there were no Jewish surgeons in North City; in 1957, there were eight. Among the country club physicians are specialists in internal medicine, allergies, and ear, nose, and throat ailments.[4]

The large majority of these doctors' patients are Jewish, although the proportion of non-Jews among them is growing as affiliation with Mount Sinai Hospital increases chances for obtaining non-Jewish patients. Many physicians consider their professional prestige improved by greater contacts with gentile doctors and patients. Others suspect that their real status lies in serving Jewish patients, whose in-group sentiments are exploitable in dollars and cents. One knowledgeable physician explains, "Jews will spend any amount of money necessary to be cured, gentiles will not." Some doctors, therefore, fear that an increase in gentile patients would mean a decrease in income. (Whether or not Jewish doctors in North City do earn more than gentile doctors is not known.)

Most local medical men have their offices in the Medical Arts Building, whose downtown location is attractive for its convenient proximity to the business and shopping area. Some, however, prefer to maintain offices in their places of residence, a practice that is prestigeful only when the neighborhood is a fashionable one.

The status of Jewish lawyers in North City is also ambiguous because of their traditional (and involuntary) location in the more risky and less prestigeful areas of the profession. Usually they are in independent practice, handling cases of negligence or crime for a preponderantly Jewish clientele. However, with the postwar industrial expansion and subsequent growth of the city, they have been employed in-

4. One local physician is known colloquially in Jewish circles as the "nose doctor" thanks to his particular in-group specialty. He is most frequently called upon to practice his plastic skills on the "too Jewish" noses of marriageable young women.

creasingly by various industries and real estate firms, most
of which are Jewish. Among the legal set in Pinecrest are
specialists in real estate, corporate, and criminal law.

The problems of Jewish dentists in North City are not
unlike those of doctors and lawyers. They are even more
likely to have only Jewish patients and complain of exclusion
from office in local dental societies. The consequence noted
by one of their spokesmen is that Jewish dentists "keep too
much to themselves." This last angry dentist argues that
Jews enter dentistry because of the promise of financial
reward, unlike gentiles, who are motivated by genuine professional interest. It is his acidulous opinion that Jewish
dentists are "misplaced businessmen" who have introduced
the ethic of profit into the profession and thus alienated
themselves from non-Jewish dentists.

The country club professionals have relatively high incomes ranging from $15,000 to $25,000 a year. These figures
may be understated, however, because of the public lip
service that is paid to humanitarian, rather than materialistic
norms. Lawyers have the highest and dentists the lowest
incomes; the financial position of lawyers is probably due
to their connection with profitable business and real estate
interests.

Denied the pleasures of collegial social circles, Jewish
professionals in North City are more sensitive to the judgments of other Jews than to those of professional peers. The
minority group supplants the profession as a status audience.
Although professional status communities value professional
achievement, the upper-middle-class businessmen with
whom Jewish professionals associate value material achievement. Professional values, therefore, have been displaced by
the nonprofessional standards of those who are willing to
accord social recognition to Jewish professionals.

The Difference Money Makes

The class differences between clubniks and lodgniks are reflected in their respective styles of life; the importance of money lies in the material comforts it affords. (See Table 3.) Spending begins at home and economic contrasts show up in the nature of home ownership. Although the majority of both clubniks and lodgniks own their own homes, the average house value for the former is $33,593 in contrast to $13,833 for the latter. While lodgniks remain clustered in the area of first settlement, clubniks have long been dispersed throughout the more expensive south and west neighborhoods.

Like all *nouveaux riches*, club members unabashedly enjoy their means, living up to the great expectations of their income in everything money can buy. Their conspicuous consumption is matched only by their conspicuous charity; they give as generously as they buy extravagantly. Much of their social lives can be subsumed under these organizing principles of status. Clubniks, for example, own two cars in the Cadillac and Lincoln class, and take extended (and expensive) vacations at resort hotels or abroad. Their clothes are custom-made, their cigars hand-rolled, their whiskey well-aged. The less endowed lodgniks, economically removed from the gilded ghetto, must be content with lesser luxuries: Fords and Chevrolets, vacations at home, ready-made clothes.

Even the education of country club children is more expensive. They attend private secondary schools and the Ivy League colleges of the east coast. More children of club members are entering their fathers' businesses or similar occupations in contrast to the children of lodge members, who are entering different occupations from those of their fathers. Obviously, it is the clubniks who have the successful businesses to pass on to their children. Without this dubious advantage, children of lodgniks actually have more career alternatives from which to choose.

Not ones to lag behind their non-Jewish peers in anything, clubniks belong to many organizations, at least as dues-paying members.[5] In fact, they belong to twice as many organizations as do lodgniks, whose lives are more circumscribed by the boundaries of the neighborhood. The cost of so many membership fees, especially those of the exclusive social clubs, is beyond the means of lodgniks. Members of the country club, in contrast, are able to enjoy the things that cost money and enhance their prestige, even in the eyes of the less privileged lodgniks.

These are the ways in which the horizontal principles of economic class cut across the Jewish community, producing within it class and status differences analogous to those found in the general community. Such contrasts occur in both Jewish and non-Jewish behavior. These class factors, however, do link Jews to the institutions of the wider society. Jews respond to the influences of class from within the institutional contexts of the minority community. Much of the social differentiation among Jews stems from the stratification system indigenous to the Jewish community itself. The specifically ethnic differences that stratify the community reflect uniquely "Jewish" characteristics.

5. Evidence of the extensive social participation of the upper classes is presented in Mirra Komarovsky, "The Voluntary Associations of Urban Dwellers," *American Sociological Review*, *11*, 686–98 and Leonard Reissman, "Class, Leisure and Social Participation," *American Sociological Review*, *19*, 76–84.

5

What Money Can't Buy

MUCH OF THE STATUS behavior of North City Jews occurs
in a context peculiar to the traditional subculture of the
Jewish community. The stratification of the in-group is
based on differential access to specifically Jewish values as
well as to general values. These traditional Jewish values
have their origin in the ethnic, religious, and class characteristics of Eastern European immigrants. The values that
emerged in the ghetto milieu of orthodox piety and poverty
have since been modified by the class-linked response of the
second generation to its minority-group status in American
society.

The mingling of class and ethnic values makes it difficult
to ascertain their relative influence in order to distinguish
between Jewish life styles and those of non-Jews of similiar
social and economic background. Although difficult to define independently, these values are linked to the institutional
structure of the minority community and determine the
characteristic responses of Jews to their life situation. It is
these responses which, in turn, form the structure of the
contemporary Jewish community, providing a social definition of *Jewish* patterns of behavior. Derived from many
sources, these patterns of behavior are part of a social structure that is broadly subcultural rather than specifically religious.

"Jewish" values (whether economic or religious in origin)

thus refer to the values and patterns of behavior traditionally associated with the segregated ethnic community, while "non-Jewish" values refer to those associated with the dominant society. An analysis of the relationship between the uniquely Jewish stratification system and the differential access to dominant values enjoyed by various strata of Jews requires study of the relative acceptance and rejection of traditional Jewish values.

CONTRASTS IN ETHNIC STATUS CHARACTERISTICS

The hypothesis concerning second-generation status behavior predicts that the higher the status in the Jewish community, the greater the acceptance of non-Jewish values and the less the acceptance of traditional Jewish values. Table 4 summarizes the major contrasts in status (not predictable from economic differences alone) between club members and lodge members. The presentation of the data on the distribution of Jewish and non-Jewish values proceeds from institutional patterns to interpersonal relations.

Religion. In American society, the class and status factors that stratify the dominant religion of Protestantism also stratify the minority religion of Judaism. The difference is, of course, that the stratification of Judaism occurs within the institutional context of a separate community. The major branches of American Judaism—Reform, Conservative, and Orthodox—are as much the product of stratification by class and status factors as they are of differences in theology.

Both clubniks and lodgniks are synagogue members, but the specific affiliation varies with social class.[1] Club members

1. Cf. Liston Pope's classic study of the relationship between church affiliation and class membership, *Millhands and Preachers* (New Haven, Yale University Press, 1945). There is analogous, if inconclusive, evidence that shifts in synagogue affiliation are as-

TABLE 4. Ethnic Status Characteristics of
Pinecrest Club and Silverman Lodge

VARIABLE	Per Cent of Club	Per Cent of Lodge	Significance of Difference *
1. Belong to Reform Temple	66.0	0.0	Significant
2. Attend synagogue on High Holidays only	78.0	52.0	Significant
3. Observe kosher laws	0.0	18.0	Significant
4. Wife non-Jewish	8.0	0.0	Significant
5. Children attend Talmud Torah	34.0	88.0	Significant
6. Anglo-Saxon surname	28.0	0.0	Significant
7. Give children Anglo-Saxon names	50.0	6.0	Significant
8. Vacation at non-Jewish resorts	16.0	10.0	Significant
9. Have Christmas tree	26.0	4.0	Significant
10. Belong to non-Jewish organizations	94.0	22.0	Significant
11. Contribute most to Jewish philanthropies	92.0	10.0	Significant *
12. Active in non-Jewish causes	86.0	8.0	Significant
13. Live in Jewish neighborhood	8.0	90.0	Significant
14. Have gentile friends	56.0	12.0	Significant

* But in a direction opposite to that predicted.

belong to the Reform synagogue and lodge members to
Orthodox and Conservative synagogues. (See Table 5.)

The Reform synagogue in North City serves an upper-
class Jewish congregation whose membership includes the
wealthiest professionals and businessmen in the community.
A Jew joins the "Temple" when he wishes to become as

sociated with changes in status. In this study, for example, there
are a number of cases of movement from Orthodox and Conservative synagogues to the Reform Temple upon improvement of the
individuals' financial circumstances.

TABLE 5. Synagogue Membership of Pinecrest Club and Silverman Lodge

| | CLUB | | LODGE | |
	Number	Per Cent	Number	Per Cent
Orthodox	0	0	14	28
Reform	33	66	0	0
Conservative	17	34	36	72
Total	50	100	50	100

chi-square = 56.6   P = .01   T = .75 *

* The nature of our statistical analysis follows from the logic of the theoretical framework and the substantive hypotheses derived from it. The first part of the study is concerned with the predicted association of certain social characteristics with membership in particular status groups. The occurrence of various behavioral attributes among high-status Jews is therefore compared with their occurrence among low-status Jews. The chi-square test is the most appropriate one for ascertaining the significance of differences between high- and low-status groups. The same test is also used in the second part of the study to test the relationship between membership in a generation and certain social characteristics.

For purposes of statistical testing, the substantive hypotheses are restated as null hypotheses, predicting *no* relationship between status (or generation) and behavioral variables. The chi-square test then determines whether the difference between the theoretically expected frequencies and the empirically observed frequencies is explainable by chance, or if the difference is large enough to reject the null hypothesis. This statistic indicates only the existence (or nonexistence) of an association between variables. The content and direction of the relationship is specified by the theoretical framework of the study. Chi-square determines whether or not the null hypothesis is to be rejected, but our theory determines the nature of the substantive hypothesis.

Because chi-square varies greatly with sample size, it can reveal the existence of a relationship between variables, but not the degree of association. Tschuprow's coefficient is used to measure the amount of association in tables with more than four cells and phi-square is used in fourfold tables. Although these measures of socially successful as he is economically successful. Most Pinecrest members belong to the Reform Temple and share with their fellow congregants social as well as religious values. The Orthodox and Conservative synagogues to which Silverman members belong have middle- and lower-class congregations whose members are workingmen, craftsmen, and small proprietors from the less well endowed socioeconomic strata of the Jewish community. As synagogues of the first generation, many of them remain more traditional and less social in orientation than the Reform Temple. Most of them are neighborhood synagogues located on the North Side. The Reform Temple stands alone in a non-Jewish neighborhood on the South Side.

As a further check on the relationship between class and religious affiliation, the type of synagogue membership was cross-tabulated with income level within the two sample groups. In the lodge, the higher-income individuals are Conservative and the lower-income individuals are Orthodox. (See Table 6.) In the club, the higher-income individuals are Reform and the lower-income individuals Conservative. (See Table 7.) The Conservative synagogue provides the one social setting in which clubniks and lodgniks may associate with one another in a more intimate manner than is customary between the two strata. As a result, it is the most socially heterogeneous of the three branches of Judaism. Because of this heterogeneity, there is some differentia-

---

association are not entirely adequate, they give some indication of the theoretical significance of statistically significant relationships. Relationships are accepted as significant at the .05 level of confidence or beyond in this study, but the statistical level of significance is not necessarily a sufficient index of the substantive importance of a relationship. (For the logic of the statistical argument used throughout the study see Roy G. Francis, "Statistical Methods" in *An Introduction to Social Research*, John Doby et al., eds. (Harrisburg, Pa., Stackpole, 1954).

TABLE 6. Synagogue Membership and Income Level
in Silverman Lodge

| | ORTHODOX | | CONSERVATIVE | |
	Number	Per Cent	Number	Per Cent
$3,000–5,999	12	24	13	26
$6,000–20,000	2	4	23	46
Total	14	28	36	72

chi-square = 9.9   P = .01   phi = .44

tion within Conservatism. Although there is only one
Reform synagogue in North City, there are two major
Conservative synagogues (and a new one recently established in West Parricus). One, on the North Side, is the
synagogue to which most Conservative lodge members belong. The South Side congregation is the one to which most
Conservative Pinecrest members belong.

TABLE 7. Synagogue Membership and Income Level
in Pinecrest Club

| | CONSERVATIVE | | REFORM | |
	Number	Per Cent	Number	Per Cent
$10,000–25,999	14	28	11	22
$26,000–50,000	3	6	22	44
Total	17	34	33	66

chi-square = 12.0   P = .01   phi = .38

Differences in membership costs are not sufficiently great
to account for the economic stratification of the North City
synagogues. Status considerations combine with financial
ones to create the characteristic milieu of each synagogue;
members prefer to be able to afford the accepted style of
life of their fellow congregants. A prospective member of
the Reform Temple considers not only the membership fee,
but the cost of keeping up with the Reform Joneses.

For many clubniks, synagogue affiliation (of a particular kind) represents a social requirement of their socioeconomic stratum. Their reasons for affiliating with one synagogue or another are "strategic" ones, i.e., they are formulated in terms of opportunities provided by a given congregation for meeting socially prominent people and making contacts for business purposes. The lodgniks offer such "traditional" reasons as: it's always been done, all good Jews should belong, and it's good for the children. Apparently, appropriate synagogue affiliation is more critical for upwardly mobile clubniks than the more immobile lodgniks.

The religious contrasts between the club and the lodge do not end with synagogue affiliation; there are also differences in religious behavior. Club members attend synagogue less frequently than lodge members, with 78 per cent of the former appearing only on the High Holidays in comparison to 48 per cent of the latter. They also observe less ritual than lodge members. Eighty-six per cent of the clubniks acknowledge their religious tradition with nothing more than occasional Sabbath candles and Passover seders, while the lodgniks adhere to more demanding practices. For example, the most discriminating difference between the two groups is the observance of the dietary laws. None of the club members adhere to them, but 24 per cent of the lodge members observe at least some of these laws. Many lodge members buy only kosher meat; none in the club does so. This does not mean that in contrast to club members, lodge members are strictly kosher. Actually no lodge members are kosher in the orthodox sense (keeping two sets of dishes, eating no pork products, mixing no meat and milk products), but some retain the traditional practice of buying only kosher meat and fish. The social significance of even this token observance is its tendency to discourage table community with gentiles and thus limit intimate social interaction with them.

Adherence to religious commandments can impose many restrictions on the social behavior of Jews. Seeking more association with the gentile community, Pinecrest members find traditional religious practices particularly constraining. With the disappearance of the first generation, even lodge members are observing less and less of the orthodoxy of their fathers. However, they are still able to observe more ritual than club members, since their religious practices are supported by their basic social commitment to the Jewish community and its traditional values. Club members, on the other hand, are socially committed to both the Jewish and non-Jewish communities and must tread a fine line that violates the religious values of neither. Ironically, country clubbers often find that the religious observance that offends some of their Jewish associates wins them the respect of non-Jews.

The most persistent religious injunction has been against intermarriage. Traditionally, a Jew who marries a non-Jew risks ritual defilement and social ostracism. The increasing acculturation of the Jewish community has rendered ineffective many of its religious sanctions, and the proscription against intermarriage has lost much of its capacity for social control. The general impression is that the rate of Jewish intermarriage in North City has been increasing, but there are only two cases of intermarriage among our respondents, both in Pinecrest Club and both instances of Jewish men marrying Protestant wives. The country club, however, includes in its social circles more intermarried couples than does the lodge. Although intermarriage is not too frequent in the club, it is accepted, if not explicitly approved. Lodge members know of relatively few intermarriages and disapprove of them in principle. In most cases of intermarriage, conflict over religious issues has been by-passed by raising the children as Jews.

Neither club nor lodge members reject the traditional value of religious education, but the content has been considerably watered down, and the value weakened, in one group. Sixty-six per cent of club members' children receive minimum or Sunday School instruction only, while 88 per cent of lodge members' children receive maximum or Talmud Torah (Hebrew School) instruction. The types of religious education differ in the number of days a week instruction is given. Sunday School meets only once a week, while Talmud Torah meets five times a week, prompting a high-ranking Conservative rabbi to complain that the Talmud Torah monopolizes Jewish education in North City. The afternoons of Pinecrest children are occupied with junior versions of country club activities as well as music and dancing lessons. There is no time left for daily religious instruction.

Sunday Schoolers lack the interest and opportunity to learn in the traditional fashion of the Talmud Torah, whose students derive status from scholarly achievement. Graduation from Talmud Torah is an important occasion, signifying the attainment of a certain level of sacred knowledge. Religious education, highly esteemed by lodgniks, has no comparable value for clubniks. Club members value more secular achievement, favoring particularly the cultivation of various social skills. Yet, many attribute whatever religious observance they practice to the influence of their children's Sunday schooling. One clubnik complained peevishly, "The rabbi gets our kids in the palm of his hand and sends them home to make us feel ashamed of being irreligious Jewish parents."

Education. The value of secular learning continues to be honored among Jews, but in a way that is differentiated by class and status. Clubniks and lodgniks, for example, favor different types of education. As indicated above, 22 per cent of the club members send their children to private schools, while no lodge member does so.

Private secondary schools have special social significance for Jewish children. These hallowed institutions are predominantly non-Jewish and afford young Jews opportunities to associate with gentile social peers. Prep schools offer anticipatory socialization for entry into the more exclusive clubs and fraternities of the Ivy League. It is a critical qualification for social success in private colleges that Jewish students ordinarily lack. The absence of prep school background has been systematically used against Jewish applicants for membership in exclusive Ivy League societies.[2] Pinecrest children graduating from private schools thus have some advantage over public school graduates in overcoming the social drawbacks of their Jewish identity. Lacking these alternatives, the children of lodge members have different problems. Their channel of mobility is through academic rather than social achievement; they are more likely to sacrifice the social graces for high grades.

The characteristic Jewish pattern of higher education seems prevalent in both club and lodge; over 90 per cent of the children in both groups attend college. There is a difference, however, in the colleges attended. Private eastern colleges are more highly esteemed than local colleges by the upper socioeconomic strata of North City. They can be particularly valuable to Jewish boys desiring access to more diverse and prestigeful social circles than exist locally. The Ivy League plays an equally important role for Jewish girls as a source of more socially eligible husbands than are available locally.

By and large, higher education provides the vocational training necessary for mobility. Most children enter differ-

2. See Walter Goodman, "Bicker at Princeton," *Commentary*, *24*, 406–15.

ent occupations from those of their fathers.[3] (See Table 8.) In general, the children of club members go into business and those of lodge members the professions. This is all the more striking when it is recalled that most of the established professionals in the sample are in the club. (Their children

TABLE 8. Businessmen and Professionals among the Children of Pinecrest Club and Silverman Lodge

| | CLUB | | LODGE | |
	Number	*Per Cent*	*Number*	*Per Cent*
Professionals	20	48	36	78
Businessmen	22	52	10	22
Total *	42	100	46	100

chi-square = 8.9   P = .01   phi = .29

* 12 responses omitted due to lack of children or females without careers.

have also entered the professions, although not necessarily the same ones as their fathers.) The small retailers and craftsmen of the lodge, who can rarely provide more than moral support for their sons, turn out an unexpectedly high number of professionals. This pattern is not new; the fathers of the professionals in the sample were also craftsmen and small proprietors. The children of wealthier Jewish families are more likely to enter family businesses or establish their own. Within the Jewish community, the professions remain a channel of mobility frequently employed by the lower strata.

Naming Patterns. Those who would be upwardly mobile must at some point be willing to relinquish an old way of life for a new one. Consequently, the anticipation of mobility may lead to a transformation of social identity, brought

3. To obtain comparable data, the characteristics of only the oldest child were included in the statistical analysis.

about, in part, by a change of name. This pattern of name-changing occurs particularly in a society in which a negative evaluation is attached to names associated with minority group background.

Jews, for example, change their names as a means of ridding themselves of at least one symbol of their "Jewishness." [4] Lengthy names like Hershkowitz and Moskowitz are easily shortened to Hersh and Moss. Other names, like Rubenstein, Epstein, and Greenberg, are changed to such nondescript names of presumed Anglo-Saxon origin as Rayburn, Evans, and Gilmore. The latter pattern, rather than the retention of a typically Jewish, but shortened name, is the more significant one in a consideration of status.[5]

In America, allegedly typical Jewish surnames are derived (with some variation) from Eastern and Central European Jewish nomenclature. Although some of these names were Anglicized as families migrated to Western Europe and America, they retained their identifiable character. Goldberg and Bernstein have German origins, just as Berkowitz and Kashinsky have Polish and Russian origins. But in American society, these names label persons of Jewish ancestry.

None of the lodgniks has an Anglo-Saxon surname. The twenty-eight per cent of the clubniks with non-Jewish names are those who enjoy particularly high prestige among their Jewish peers and frequent interaction with gentiles.

4. Of course aesthetic values play some part in Jewish name-changing. Such names as Lewis and Rose "sound better" than Lipschitz or Rosenzweig. For a study of name-changing see Leonard Broom, "Characteristics of 1107 Petitioners for Change of Name," *American Sociological Review, 20,* 33–42.

5. Judgments about the identity of specific names were made on the basis of J. Alvin Kugelmass, "Name Changing and What It Gets You," *Commentary, 18,* 105–14; Albert Gordon, *Jews in Transition* (Minneapolis, University of Minnesota Press, 1945), pp. 318–20.

Actually, they have changed their names more out of eagerness to insure membership in the exclusive circles of "non-Jewish" Jews than out of desire to shed their Jewishness. Name-changing is not acceptable to all strata of Jews. As long as lodgniks remain in their present social position, they gain no advantage from changing their names. The practice is objectionable to them, and they reject anyone who does change his name, explaining, "Jews who change their names are just ashamed of being Jewish. We should be proud of being Jewish." [6]

The kind of first name given children also varies in American society, revealing differences between Jews and non-Jews. A recent survey by George Gallup of the given names most popular in the United States during the past few decades reveals shifts in popularity for a series of male and female names. The listing includes only a few of the names which have been most common among Jewish families during the same time. Such names as John, Thomas, James, Charles, Joseph, Patricia, Catherine, Margaret, Elizabeth, and Mary won favor in the general society during the past two decades. During the same period such names as Sheldon, Harvey, Norman, Bernard, Howard, Rhoda, Gloria, Sheila, Muriel, and Marilyn were favorites among Jews. More recently some overlap has developed, with such names as Karen, Linda, Deborah, Eric, Michael, and Stephen popular among both Jews and non-Jews.

6. It might come as a surprise to both clubniks and lodgniks to learn that the Talmud recognizes the connection between a person's name and his soul (or self). Ironically, it sanctions a change of given name, although not for invidious purposes of status. The name of a critically ill person may be changed as one way of changing his fate. (Other ways elaborated by the Talmud are prayer, charity, and good works.) The origin of this custom is traced to the Old Testament in which, for example, Sarai's name is changed to Sarah, after which it is stated that "she shall be blessed."

Many of the old stand-bys such as Helen, Dorothy, Frances, Alice, Henry, Harry, Frank, Albert, and Louis have dropped from the top of the list. Similarly, many of the once-popular names among Jews such as Isaac, Irving, Isadore, Abraham, Sara, Miriam, and Bertha have fallen into disuse in recent years. However, there appears to be a revival among *both* Jews and gentiles of such "old-fashioned" Biblical names as Rebecca, Rachel, Shulamith, Raphael, and Ephraim,[7] permitting Jews to use the Old Testament as a source of nomenclature without loss of status.

Children of clubniks are more likely to have Anglo-Saxon names than children of lodgniks. Furthermore, Pinecrest children with non-Jewish surnames are also likely to have non-Jewish given names. (See Table 9.) They constitute a stratum of young Jews with an important non-Jewish char-

TABLE 9. Surnames and Given Names of Children of Pinecrest Club *

	JEWISH GIVEN NAMES		ANGLO-SAXON GIVEN NAMES	
	Number	Per Cent	Number	Per Cent
Jewish surnames	23	46	2	4
Anglo-Saxon surnames	6	12	19	38
	29		21	

chi-square = 29.9   P = .01   phi = .71

* The picture presented here is probably a conservative one since only eldest children are included, and many families, after naming their first-born traditionally, feel free to name their younger offspring less traditionally.

7. See Ben zion E. Kaganoff, "Jewish First Names Through the Ages," *Commentary*, 20, 249–59. For purposes of analysis we have regarded the following as Jewish names: Howard, Norman, Sheldon, Marvin, Gloria, Marilyn, Beverly, and Muriel; these were included among the non-Jewish or Anglo-Saxon names: Thomas, James, Andrew, Morgan, Elizabeth, Catherine, Patricia, and Margaret.

acteristic, an Anglo-Saxon name. They attend private schools and eastern colleges, which contribute to their socialization as "personable" young Jews, Jews, that is, with non-Jewish social traits. They lack no confidence about obtaining jobs that will lead to social success. In this expectation their parents more than concur; they do everything they can to bring about its realization. The motivating force of this image of a new and non-Jewish way of life is a powerful one.

These naming patterns then are part of the plan of farsighted parents who hope their children will enjoy the advantages of non-Jewish social circles. Parents preparing for a better future will first change their family name and then give their children non-Jewish first names, providing them with a potentially non-Jewish identity. This new identity may not be needed, but it is at least available for participating in non-Jewish circles or applying for jobs or club memberships from which Jews are excluded.

Giving non-Jewish names to children represents a break with the tradition of naming newborn children after deceased grandparents (or other relatives). The name need not be the same as that of the particular relative in question, but it is usually similar (or at least begins with the same letter). While such names as Jerry and Jack have been acceptable derivatives of Jacob, John and James have not. (Some years ago a noted rabbi who named his newborn son James was criticized in many Jewish social circles.) Although there are now Jewish children called James and John, high-status Jews sometimes compromise with the past by naming their first-born in the traditional manner and the younger children in nontraditional fashion. This is, in fact, the pattern among club members.

Style of Life. As it is possible to identify Jewish (and non-Jewish) names, so it is possible to identify life styles that emerge from class-linked, but uniquely Jewish responses to minority-group status. These life styles do not represent specific Jewish (or non-Jewish) values so much as the characteristic social responses of Jews to their situation. Thus, there are Jewish vacations, Jewish tastes in clothing, Jewish uses of leisure time. For example, on the rare occasions when lodge members spend their vacations at resorts, they patronize the ones catering to a Jewish clientele. Club members vacation at resorts more frequently, and 16 per cent choose those with non-Jewish guests.

The social situation of the resort hotel derives its special character from the "sociability" of its patrons and their relations as status equals. The relative isolation of the resort from the outside world encourages social interdependence among the guests, who develop at least a transient status community in which the members accept one another on more or less equal terms.

Resort situations thus offer Jews a unique chance for social intercourse with gentiles based upon mutual esteem to an extent rarely possible in the workaday world. As a guest at a non-Jewish resort, a Jew may wine and dine with gentiles, experiences which he prizes but rarely enjoys in his ordinary social life. A vacation at a Jewish resort hotel may be as expensive, or more so, than one at a non-Jewish resort. It may also include such attractive features as traditional Jewish foods served in large quantities and elaborate recreational facilities such as card rooms and professional entertainment. In fact, most second-generation Jews prefer a perennial return to the familiarity of the Jewish resort to experimenting with the strange status audience of a new resort. They can play the social game with ease at a Jewish resort, engaging in a conspicuous display of wealth with people who play by the same rules. It is the non-Jewish resorts, however, that create the social conditions for peer relations with gentiles. Those Jews willing to risk the unknown stand to enhance their status after the holiday is over.

Second-generation Jews have typically demonstrated more prowess at the card table than on the playing fields. Only recently, for example, have Jews begun to play golf, long defined as a gentile sport. "The Christians have played golf for two hundred years and it takes years to learn the etiquette of the game." [8] Golf is now the most popular sport among country clubbers. They take pride in their course, of which "no Jew has to be ashamed when he invites gentiles for a day of golf and liquid refreshment." Pinecrest claims a monopoly on the "way golf should be played." The importance of the private course lies in its prestigeful aura of gentile golfing folkways. Bowling, the most popular sport among lodgniks, is scorned by clubniks as a lower-class sport.

As patrons of the arts, some club members are now participating in activities once jealously guarded as the exclusive domain of the non-Jewish elite. Sponsoring concert series and art museums is becoming *de rigeur* among upper-status Jews as they learn the status value of these activities. Involvement in the arts may lead to the kind of association with gentiles that develops more readily between people with common interests than between representatives of different communities.

In keeping with the difference in their incomes, clubniks' taste in clothing is conservative and more expensive than that of lodgniks. They patronize custom and exclusive ready-made shops, whereas lodge members shop at department stores and two-price Jewish stores. Bargaining with Jewish shopkeepers is a popular pastime among lodgniks. The joy of the barter, the pride of the outcome is not granted to the *goyishe kopf*, who doesn't know a

8. See W. Lloyd Warner and Leo Srole, *The Social Systems of American Ethnic Groups* (New Haven, Yale University Press, 1945), p. 88.

bargain when he sees one. The salesman, meeting customer resistance within the in-group, counters with, "Do you want a *goy* should get such a good coat?" On the other hand, in an effort to avoid the offensive role of "Fagin with a tape measure," the Jewish merchant may actually permit members of the out-group to drive a harder bargain than *landsmann*. Although the quality, styles, and prices of two-price stores differ from those of non-Jewish stores, the reason high-status Jews avoid them is the characteristic haggling they consider a uniquely Jewish vice. They have traded the Jewish bargain for non-Jewish courtesy.

Christmas Observance. Another interesting in-group pattern is the way in which Jews observe Christmas. Although Christmas is a specifically Christian holiday, there are nonreligious aspects of the holiday acknowledged by acculturated Jews. Three measures of Christmas observance were considered: sending cards, which was considered minimum or ordinary (Jewish) observance, and having trees and exchanging gifts within the immediate family, considered maximum or more than ordinary observance (for Jews).

Club members send more cards than do lodge members. (See Table 10.) Both groups send more cards to gentiles

TABLE 10. Christmas Card Sending by Pinecrest Club and Silverman Lodge

	CLUB		LODGE	
	Number	*Per Cent*	*Number*	*Per Cent*
Send cards to Jews	28	56	11	22
Send cards to non-Jews	49	98	27	54
Send no cards	1	2	12	24
Total	78		50	

chi-square = 18.9   P = .01   T = .33

than to Jews, a strategem shared by both rich and poor businessmen alike to promote good will in the general community—and improve business. Of course, these greeting cards may also serve as a token of respect for the religious observance of Christmas. What is most interesting, however, is that over half of the clubniks send cards to other Jews, while only 22 per cent of the lodgniks do so. Lodgniks, still committed to a vestige of their sacred tradition, confine their Christmas greetings almost entirely to non-Jews; they may honor the religious practices of the dominant group, but they do not adopt them within the in-group. Among the more secularized clubniks, in contrast, the observance of certain dominant patterns of behavior has become one of the prerequisites of status.

Not to be outdone by the generosity of their gentile neighbors, both clubniks and lodgniks give and receive Christmas gifts. They differ, however, in their patterns of gift-giving. In addition to exchanging gifts with gentile businessmen, as do lodge members, club members also exchange gifts within the family (for the sake of the children, of course). (See Table 11.) The greatest shock to Silver-

TABLE 11. Christmas Observance by Pinecrest Club
and Silverman Lodge

	CLUB		LODGE	
	Number	*Per Cent*	*Number*	*Per Cent*
Tree and family gifts	13	26	2	4
No tree and no family gifts	37	74	48	96
Total	50	100	50	100

chi-square = 9.5   P = .01   phi = .31

man sensibility is the clubniks' display of the last word in Christmas symbolism, the tree. Among the country club set, the higher the income, the more likely the family is to have trees and exchange gifts (see Table 12), a finding

TABLE 12. Christmas Observance and Income Level
in Pinecrest Club

| | TREE AND GIFTS | | NO TREE AND GIFTS | |
	Number	Per Cent	Number	Per Cent
$10,000–25,999	3	8	22	42
$26,000–50,000	10	18	15	32
Total	13	26	37	74

chi-square = 5.1   P = .05   phi = .54

that contributes further evidence of an especially high-income substratum within Pinecrest whose members have more non-Jewish social traits than the club as a whole.

The observance of Christmas by these Jews helps to establish their social ties to the larger community through shared participation in the traditional rituals of the dominant society.[9] Those who fail to practice the appropriate Christmas rites may be criticized, or even ostracized, in a particular locality. As non-Christians, Jews are not religiously committed to such observance, but they may be socially and culturally committed in a society where Christmas is virtually a national holiday. Increasingly tempting to Jews, the token observance of the more secular aspects of Christmas serves as symbolic expression of identity with the larger society, reducing their uniqueness and visibility.

Organizational Membership. A distinctive feature of Jewish social life is the critical role played by organizations and clubs, most of which recruit membership only from the minority group. Jewish communities have long been characterized as "overorganized"; most of them contain proportionately more organizations than the general community.

9. For a discussion of the symbolic life of Americans, see W. Lloyd Warner, *The Living and the Dead* (New Haven, Yale University Press, 1959), especially pp. 278–9, 404–7.

The traditional exclusion of Jews from non-Jewish clubs and organizations in North City has contributed to a high rate of affiliation in Jewish organizations for both clubniks and lodgniks. There is a difference, however, in the frequency of membership in such nonsectarian organizations as the Masons, Community Chest, and Chamber of Commerce. (See Table 13.) More clubniks than lodgniks belong to non-Jewish organizations. (See Table 14.) The latter limit their memberships to such Jewish organizations as fraternal orders, Zionist groups, and synagogue men's

TABLE 13. Organizational Memberships of
Pinecrest Club and Silverman Lodge

ORGANIZATION	CLUB		LODGE	
	Number	Per Cent	Number	Per Cent
Board of Federation for Jewish Service	19	38.0	0	0.0
Board of Mount Sinai Hospital	13	26.0	0	0.0
Silverman Lodge of B'nai B'rith	0	0.0	50	100.0
Myron Blum Gilmore Lodge of B'nai B'rith	36	72.0	0	0.0
Criterion Club	38	76.0	4	8.0
Pinecrest or Riverside Country Club	50	100.0	0	0.0
Zionist Organization of America	13	26.0	23	46.0
American Automobile Association	33	66.0	7	14.0
Masons	32	64.0	7	14.0
Union or Professional Organizations	11	22.0	22	44.0
Chamber of Commerce, Community Chest, Kiwanis, and other civic organizations	28	56.0	4	8.0
	273		117	
	$\overline{X}$ 5.4		$\overline{X}$ 2.3	

96 THE SECOND GENERATION

TABLE 14. Jewish and Non-Jewish Organizational Memberships of Pinecrest Club and Silverman Lodge

	CLUB		LODGE	
	Number	*Per Cent*	*Number*	*Per Cent*
Jewish organizations only	3	6	39	78
Jewish and non-Jewish organizations	47	94	11	22
Total	50	100	50	100

chi-square = 51.9   P = .01   phi = .71

clubs. More clubniks also belong to the Automobile Association of America, which in North City functions as a country club as well as a service organization, and has only recently accepted Jews.

Jews have been more successful in gaining entry into organizations based upon norms of *inclusiveness* than those based upon norms of *exclusiveness*.[10] That is, more Jews belong to service organizations with civic functions (North State Centennial Committee or North City Aquatennial Committee) than to the more "social" organizations in which members are recruited by special invitation (e.g., Kiwanis, Rotary, or the Athletic Club). Because country clubbers are more likely to be affiliated with non-Jewish organizations, they have greater access to gentile social circles in which they may find themselves playing the role of "ambassador." In return for formal peer status, these ethnic diplomats are asked to represent the Jewish community in affairs of status (such as fund-raising, civic projects, and inter-faith activities).

10. For reasons of service to the community, or humanitarian or democratic ideals, organizations based upon norms of inclusiveness attempt to recruit as many members as possible, regardless of socioeconomic background. In contrast, organizations based upon norms of exclusiveness represent status communities and select their members according to specific social and economic qualifications.

There is consensus within each sample group about the relative prestige value of membership in various Jewish and non-Jewish organizations. Clubniks and lodgniks are both aware that membership in organizations closest to them in prestige rank has the greatest potential influence on their social standing. For example, although Pinecrest is recognized as the most prestigeful Jewish social club, lodgniks realistically claim that membership in such organizations as the Criterion Club, Riverside Country Club, and the Masons contributes more to their own social standing. As one respondent explained, "If I ever got into Pinecrest, none of my friends would have anything to do with me. Most of my friends belong to the Criterion Club, Riverside or the Masons. If I could afford to belong to those organizations, I certainly would." Silverman members were conspicuous by their failure to acknowledge the importance of the "invisible," but powerful Federation and Mount Sinai boards so salient in the strategies of high-status Jews.

Pinecrest members, lacking nothing in self-assurance, also recognize the prestige of their country club membership. But they feel that positions on the boards of the Jewish Federation and Mount Sinai and memberships in such non-Jewish organizations as the Athletic Club, museums and symphony boards, Kiwanis, Rotary, Lions, Chamber of Commerce, and Community Chest contribute the most to their social standing. Members of the high-ranking country club scorn competing Jewish clubs, such as the Riverside and Criterion Clubs, which admit low-status Jews to membership. One country clubber expressed the views of many of his fellows on these clubs: "I'm not snobbish or anything, but Riverside really has a crummy golf course and its members are people I wouldn't particularly care to associate with. As for the Criterion Club, I belong because I have to for business. But they have a

lot of undesirable elements in there now that I don't want
to have anything to do with."

There are apparently two ranking systems of club and
organizations: one for Jewish organizations and the other
for non-Jewish organizations. The lodgniks' ranking system
includes only Jewish clubs and organizations; for them,
membership in non-Jewish organizations has no bearing
on status in the Jewish community. Pinecrest membership
is regarded as the most prestigeful, but not necessarily
appropriate for them. The organizations they perceive as
influential in determining their own status are the ones
closest to them in status (e.g., Riverside and Criterion
Clubs). Membership in B'nai B'rith and the Zionist Organization of America is deemed necessary for a "good
Jew" by the lodgniks, but the social importance of such
Jewish memberships as the Federation and Mount Sinai
boards is not perceived at all. The lodge members rank
no organizations below their own, thus accepting the position of low man on the organizational totem pole.

Clubniks rank organizations differently. Their ranking
includes both Jewish and non-Jewish clubs and organizations, placing non-Jewish organizations at the top and
Jewish organizations such as B'nai B'rith and the Zionist
Organization of America at the bottom. They view their
own country club membership hopefully as a step toward
membership in non-Jewish organizations, a ploy in the
organizational status game. Ironically, the membership of
the nonsectarian organizations is likely to be drawn from
economic strata of non-Jews less affluent than Pinecrest
members. Yet membership in non-Jewish organizations
is so attractive that clubniks are willing to sacrifice economic status for the pleasures of "mixed" company. These
nonsectarian memberships do have certain economic ramifications; they may promote contacts useful for business
and professional purposes.

A special type of organizational behavior is philanthropic activity. Philanthropy has always been a legitimate way to consume wealth conspicuously. In a society in which philanthropic and fund-raising activities are highly institutionalized, the complex structure of these activities in the Jewish community does not appear particularly unique. Yet, among Jews, there is the distinctive feature of a personalized ethic of "taking care of one's own," sanctioned by religious and ethnic traditions. The structure of philanthropic activities transcends mere geography; local Jewish communities everywhere are united in protecting themselves from threat by the dominant group.

Exploiting the desire for social survival and the ever-present fear of disaster, Jewish fund-raisers maximize contributions from the in-group to an extent rarely realized in the larger community. Their techniques are so successful that their services are frequently sought by nonsectarian organizations. Only recently, however, has fund-raising among Jews become so well organized as to claim professional standing. In many communities the professional fund-raiser ranks among the highest paid personnel of Jewish social service. Power to make decisions of community-wide scope is invested in the board of the Federation and its most effective decisions are those committing the Jewish community to specific goals in its annual fund-raising drives.

Jewish philanthropic activity has become so institutionalized that it is able to regulate certain status relations within the community. Contributions are maximized when fund-raising is made a matter of community-wide concern, permitting social pressures to operate through critical status channels. Rich Jews are called upon to solicit donations from their equally rich friends because they are best able to judge how much their friends can afford to contribute. Someone less than a financial peer might be too easily impressed by any sizable amount and fail to press for more. A peculiarly invidious system has thus evolved in which friends are set upon friends to shame each other into a mounting spiral of philanthropic contributions—all for the sake of charity. What was once a religious duty has become a prerequisite of status. In a single drive, the Federation has averaged $100 per donor, the highest single contribution being $100,000.

Fund-raising is an important principle of organization in the Jewish community.[11] It has the unique function of identifying for the community all its members and involving them, however unwillingly, in the community's most intensive activity. In the Jewish social structure, philanthropic contributions are the functional equivalent of the potlatch, the Indian ceremony in which individuals give away or destroy large amounts of their property as a symbol of their status, measured by how much they can afford to waste. The more a man gives away, the higher his status and the greater the mortification of those who have been outdone.[12] Among Jews, generous gifts to worthy causes enhance a man's social honor. (This is the consequence of a charitable act, but not necessarily its motive.) The larger the donation, the higher the status of the donor.

Knowledge of the exact amount of individual donations is the special property of certain status cliques. The record is seldom made public, but the Federation keeps tabs on past contributions in order to be able to set the potlatch in motion anew each year. Efficient utilization of their knowledge of past patterns of giving permits the fund-

11. See R. M. MacIver, *Report on the Jewish Community Relations Agencies* (New York, National Community Relations Advisory Council, 1951), for evidence supporting this observation.

12. Ruth Benedict, *Patterns of Culture* (New York, Mentor Books, 1950), pp. 181–94.

raisers to mobilize and exploit all the financial resources of the community. Of course, the income of an individual sets the limits of his charitable contributions, but the fact that the mechanics of giving are socially organized raises the upper limit of his donations. The system of the philanthropic potlatch permits social pressure to maximize contributions.

The financial support of the Jewish philanthropies is greatest among the country club set. In fact, clubniks contribute proportionately more to Jewish causes than lodgniks, a finding which would seem to contradict the proposition that the lodge is the more traditional of the two groups. Presumably the lodge should contribute (proportionately) more to Jewish causes than the less traditional club. However, philanthropic contributions are more than indices of traditional Jewish values; they reflect particular life styles as well. For most North City Jews, conspicuous charity is less a matter of religious or ideological commitment than a conventional social obligation serving as a source of status.

Furthermore, philanthropic activities perform different functions for the two groups. Despite their non-Jewish behavior patterns, clubniks can afford to be "big givers" and are therefore of greater interest to fund-raisers than lodgniks. As a result, they are subject to strong pressures to maximize their contributions. They are responsive to the urging of the fund-raisers because their contributions serve to maintain ties with the Jewish community, which grants them their favored social position. The social situation of lodgniks is less favorable, but they are already securely bound to the Jewish community. They do not need to reaffirm their Jewishness, and they are not important enough to challenge the skills of the fund-raisers, who are after bigger game. For Pinecrest, Jewish philanthropic contributions constitute the one link to the Jewish community that is not attenuated, but for Silverman members, it is one of many strong ties.

Fund-raising on a volunteer basis is different from the response to professionally organized drives. As a social activity, it offers opportunities for meeting people and extending social contacts. For Jews there are two kinds of causes to raise money for: Jewish and non-Jewish, and they serve to differentiate the sample groups. Club members actively raise funds for non-Jewish causes, while lodge members are active only for Jewish causes. Clubniks especially take advantage of the chance fund-raising provides to meet gentiles. The planning and carrying through of fund drives require regular meetings of the volunteers at which there is socializing which sometimes leads to less transient associations.

Participation in non-Jewish fund-raising activities is not equally favored by all Jews. Several years ago, the Unitarian Society in North City decided to raise money for a new building. Their drive lagged seriously until an experienced (although amateur) Jewish fund-raiser was called upon to contribute his special skills. His talents bore their green fruits and the necessary funds were quickly raised, gaining for him great favor in Unitarian circles. His Jewish associates, however, were concerned that he may have given away "trade secrets" and unwittingly committed himself to non-Jewish society. "What does he mean helping those Christians build a church? What is he, one of those *goyishe* Jews or something?"

It is in the area of philanthropic activity that Pinecrest members most vividly experience the competing social forces exerted by the minority and majority communities. The amount of their financial contribution to Jewish causes is a response to pressures exerted by the Jewish community for continued participation within it. Their fund-raising activity is a response to the general community for desired social recognition and participation in it. Club members attempt to achieve equally high status in both communities, but their efforts are not always successful. Their money, after all, is still "Jewish" money.

Lodge members do not experience the same tensions. Their philanthropic activity, like all their other social activities, isolates them from the general community and encourages their exclusive participation in the Jewish community. They are subject to social forces stemming from the Jewish, rather than the general, community. Lodgniks are "little givers" whose Jewish identity is not threatened by small contributions to both the general and the Jewish community.

Another aspect of organizational behavior often involving conflicting commitments is political activity. The occasionally Republican lodgnik is particularly likely to run the gamut of conflicting political loyalties. A prosperous junkman, whose discrepancy in income and occupational status is matched only by the occasional incompatibility of his combined Republicanism and Zionism, was torn between his interests as a Jew and as a businessman when he cast his vote in the 1956 presidential election. "I'm a good Republican, but I couldn't go along with them on this Suez business, so I switched to the other guy."

Few respondents are active in political organizations, but they all express political preferences. In the 1956 national election, 40 per cent of the clubniks and 6 per cent of the lodgniks voted Republican. Formerly, however, both clubniks and lodgniks were Democrat, all having voted for Franklin D. Roosevelt. The shift in political preference in the club occurred in conjunction with improved economic circumstances. Within the club, most Republicans are found in the upper-income brackets. (See Table 15.) The special significance of the Jewish Republi-

TABLE 15. Political Preference and Income Level
in Pinecrest Club

	DEMOCRAT		REPUBLICAN	
	Number	Per Cent	Number	Per Cent
$10,000–25,999	21	42	4	8
$26,000–50,000	9	18	16	32
Total	30	60	20	40

chi-square = 12.0   P = .01   phi = .49

cans is their break with the urban, working-class tradition
of voting Democratic. Jews are now engaging in political
behavior they regard as prestigeful because of its association with the majority group, i.e., voting Republican.[13]

Friendship Patterns. The investigation of patterns of
interpersonal relations is particularly important in a study
of social stratification, since it is in the context of interpersonal relations that status is ordinarily granted. The
problem is compounded for Jews because of the distinction
they draw between Jewish and gentile friends. This social
dichotomy has come about in response to both social exclusion and traditional religious values requiring a separate
communal existence. Although Jews anticipate no difficulties in interpersonal relations with each other (as long as
they are from similar social strata), they remain wary of
intimacy with gentiles.

Friendship circles of the clubniks and lodgniks reflect
their respective social positions in the Jewish community.
A scrutiny of the characteristics of their Jewish social
circles confirms the fact that our sample groups (and their
friends) do, in fact, represent distinct social strata. The
respondents' friends live in the same neighborhoods, belong

13. See Lawrence Fuchs, *The Political Behavior of American
Jews* (Glencoe, Ill., Free Press, 1956).

to the same organizations, have much the same incomes, and are in similar occupations.

Jews still have little informal contact with gentiles in North City. The occasions on which Jews do meet gentiles include (from least to most intimate) business associations, neighborhood encounters, civic and social organization gatherings, and special social functions such as parties and dinners. Club members are more likely to have personal relations with gentiles than lodge members. (See Table 16.) Differences in social access to gentiles result largely

TABLE 16. Occasions for Meeting Gentiles—Pinecrest Club and Silverman Lodge

OCCASIONS	CLUB		LODGE	
	Number	*Per Cent*	*Number*	*Per Cent*
Business primarily	25	50.0	47	94.0
Casual neighborhood meeting	7	14.0	4	8.0
Civic and social organizations	21	42.0	2	4.0
Home parties	25	50.0	3	6.0
Weddings, funerals, Bar Mitzvahs	10	20.0	3	6.0
Total	88		59	

from differences in the business activities of clubniks and lodgniks. The craftsman or small retailer meets gentiles only across a counter that serves as both guard and symbol of the social distance between them. A professional or business executive is more likely to conduct his business at luncheon meetings, dinner parties, conventions, or the golf course. These settings contrast sharply with the impersonality of the market place and sometimes lead to meetings for purposes other than business. Because of their membership in a community of shared economic and social interests, business executives are more likely than small proprietors to carry their business associations into their social lives. Since most lodgniks are self-employed proprietors and artisans, their occupations are not a source of friendships. Consequently, they are less susceptible to the pressures of the business community and the influence of economic interests on their social lives. In contrast, clubniks enjoy more opportunities to meet gentiles under conditions in which norms of sociability operate along with those of economic rationality.

The gentile friends of the clubniks are professionals or executives drawn from strata in the general community analagous to those Pinecrest represents in the Jewish community. Even among equivalent strata, lodge members have no gentile friends. Lack of opportunity and inclination to seek friends elsewhere perpetuate the social barriers between lodgniks and gentiles.

Slightly over half the club members have gentile friends. The higher-income members of the club have more gentile friends. (See Table 17.) It is this same stratum within

TABLE 17. Number of Gentile Friends and Income Level in Pinecrest Club

	NONE OR ONE		TWO OR MORE	
	Number	*Per Cent*	*Number*	*Per Cent*
$10,000–25,999	17	77	9	32
$26,000–50,000	5	23	19	68
Total	22	100	28	100

chi-square = 7.9   P = .05   phi = .40

Pinecrest that is the most active in non-Jewish affairs and displays most of the non-Jewish characteristics of the club. Their friendships with non-Jews secure their status in the general community; their status in the Jewish community is insured by their association with Jews who also have gentile friends. Furthermore, club members are more inclined than lodge members to believe that gentile friendships contribute to their social standing in the Jewish community. Respondents who have no gentile friends do not think such friendships exert any influence on social status.

Those who accept the social importance of gentile friends are impressed with the honor accorded a Jew who knows gentiles. One country clubber explained, "Jews should honor such a person. It is about time we Jews got around and found out what *they* are like." Others added that it was the duty of the Jews to break down anti-Semitic stereotypes by "letting *them* know that we're human too." By and large, the desire for gentile friends was couched in terms of personal achievement. "I could use a few gentile friends, they'd help my business." "My friends would think I was pretty great if I had some gentile friends."

In contrast, lodgniks see no value in gentile friendships for either the community or themselves. They reject the importance of social relations with gentiles because of the futility of the outcome. The fundamental difference between Jew and gentile will never be resolved for lodge members. "Jews and gentiles, like bagels and caviar, just don't mix." "We don't need *them*, we have our own friends." What's more, "Jews are too good for gentiles." To cultivate gentile friends is considered degrading by some lodge members. "Are we ashamed of being Jewish?"

Note the reference to gentiles as "they" or "them" and Jews as "we" or "us." In commenting on friendship patterns, the respondents distinguish explicitly between the in-group and out-group.[14] And it is not only the lodge members who speak in terms of "we" and "they." Club

14. The characteristic social psychology of the in-group is embedded even in the Yiddish language. We are indebted to Natalie Joffe for pointing out that popular usage distinguishes between Jews and non-Jews by employing different verbs to describe the same behavior. Reserved for gentiles are words otherwise used in reference to animals: e.g., Jews eat (*essen*), but *goyim* eat like pigs (*fressen*); Jews die (*starben*), but *goyim* die like dogs (*pagern*); Jews take a drink (*trinken*), but *goyim* drink like sots (*soifen*).

members also share the in-group ideology and use these designations. Perhaps they are aware of something less than full acceptance by gentiles. Nevertheless, the club members' positive evaluation of gentile associations leads them to act in a way that will increase their chances for such friendships. Lodge members, on the other hand, do not seek this main chance; they continue to regard gentiles as if they belonged to an enemy camp beyond the pale of friendship.

Lodge members have met most of their friends through neighborhood contacts, which play a more significant role in their social lives than they do for clubniks, for whom organizations have a greater importance. Lodge members have lived in the same predominantly Jewish neighborhood for a number of years, a community in which the residents exchange frequent visits with one another. Many of their old friends are also their neighbors. Even lodge members, however, acknowledge the increasing importance of organizations as a source of social life.

Having met most of their friends in organizations, club members complain that they know relatively few of the residents in their neighborhoods. They don't exchange visits with neighbors unless they have already met them in other social contexts. This, in part, reflects the relatively short period of time club members have lived in their predominantly non-Jewish neighborhoods. More importantly, the absence of neighboring reflects a way of life in which business and organizational interests represent more of a community than the neighborhood. Club members are living in a society in which interests rather than birth or proximity form the basis of social organization.

Club members have also met most of their gentile friends through organizations. Clubniks, as a matter of fact, do not feel socially accepted by their gentile neighbors unless they have already met as members of the same organizations. They complain of the social barriers erected in the evening by gentiles with whom they have done business during the day. Since clubniks have met most of their gentile friends in clubs and organizations, it is small wonder that they view these memberships as a key to social acceptance.

The neighborhood remains important, however, as a symbol of a style of life. In accord with their respective values, club and lodge members prefer different neighborhoods and attribute different qualities to them. Lodge members look for good housing in the moderately priced suburbs of Silver Hills and West Parricus. They want predominantly Jewish neighborhoods populated by "nice friendly people" with whom they seek to recreate the Jewish *gemutlichkeit* of the North Side. They want to improve the quality of their housing without giving up their good neighbor policy.

Now that it is within their financial and social means, clubniks are tempted by the once forbidden fruit of neighborhoods previously closed to Jews. Especially attractive are the more expensive and less Jewish areas near Indian Lake and such suburbs west of West Parricus as Woodmere and Bristol. Country clubbers worry lest their now exclusive neighborhoods become "too Jewish" and lose their prestige value. A few Jewish neighbors make a neighborhood comfortable; too many turn it into a ghetto. Areas once considered elegant have lost status with the influx of *nouveaux riches* emigrés from the North Side. When a neighborhood becomes "too Jewish," it is time for club members to move on. "When we first moved here, it was a nice quiet gentile neighborhood. But now this noisy North Side element is coming in and frankly we want to move away."

New areas of Jewish settlement in North City vary in character according to the class and status positions of the Jews moving into them. In general, high-status Jews look for more expensive housing in outlying areas with few Jews.

Low-status Jews live in or close to the city in less expensive housing surrounded by a high proportion of Jews. High-status neighborhoods are less likely to constitute a community (for Jews) than low-status neighborhoods; the social life of the residents of the former is confined to business and organizational activities. The latter, in contrast, function as a community in which frequent social interaction occurs among neighbors.

Status Criteria. Sensitive to status distinctions, respondents ranked the three most important status criteria in the Jewish and general communities respectively. Their rankings reflect their own perceptions of the values underlying their status behavior and are treated as data rather than as theoretically determined criteria of prestige.

There is a high correlation between the rankings of club-niks and lodgniks of the status criteria most important in the Jewish community: income, work for Jewish causes, and membership in clubs and organizations. There is a low correlation, however, for the rankings of the criteria most important in the general community. The three criteria accounting for the discrepancy in these rankings are "how well the family lives" (ranked 8.5 by the club and first by the lodge), "work for community-wide causes" (ranked first by the club and eighth by the lodge), and "who your friends are" (ranked seventh by the club and 4.5 by the lodge). (See Table 18.)

The agreement of both sample groups on the most important criteria of status in the Jewish community is unexpected. On other issues, clubniks and lodgniks indicate a commitment to different social values and a concomitant variation in perception. Perhaps there is consensus on the criteria of the presumed status system in the Jewish community and variation in the criteria accepted by a particular stratum. Or perhaps their shared perception reflects a social

TABLE 18. Rank Order by Pinecrest Club and Silverman Lodge of Status Criteria of the Jewish and General Community

CRITERIA	CLUB				LODGE			
	Jewish		General		Jewish		General	
	Score	Rank	Score	Rank	Score	Rank	Score	Rank
Income	31	1	18	4	38	1	19	4.5
Work for Jewish causes	27	2	4	8.5	35	2	11	7
Membership in clubs and organizations	26	3	21	2	24	4	20	3
How well the family lives	15	4.5	4	8.5	25	3	26	1
Occupation	15	4.5	15	6	8	0	4	9
Who friends are	13	6	8	7	10	5	19	4.5
Education	10	7	16	5	6	7	13	6
Work for community-wide causes	9	8	42	1	1	9.5	10	8
Childrens' educational and occupational accomplishments	2	9.5	1	10	2	8	3	10
Who gentile friends are	2	9.5	19	3	1	9.5	25	2

1. rho—.05—Club's Jewish and general
2. rho—.30—Lodge's Jewish and general
3. rho—.92—Club and lodge Jewish
4. rho—.20—Club and lodge general

reality. Both rich and poor can agree on the importance of money.

The differences in perception of general values are particularly significant. While club members emphasize status criteria in the general community involving interpersonal relations with non-Jews, lodge members stress a style of life disengaged from interpersonal relationships. The rankings may well be rationalizations or ideological conceptions of what ought to be rather than what actually is. But whatever they are, they both influence and reflect the social behavior of the club members and lodge members. The former actually do have more personal relationships with non-Jews than the latter. The comfortable in-group existence of both clubniks and lodgniks serves as a buffer between them and the outside world. In spite of their insularity, however, they have learned one of the sociological facts of life. What confers status in one community may not do so in the other.

Last Rites. The funerals described at the end of the previous chapter can now be reinterpreted in terms of the findings. Contrasting class and ethnic tensions experienced by second-generation North City Jews were especially well illustrated in the eulogies to the deceased. Robbins was depicted as a person who had successfully overcome the handicaps of being Jewish in a gentile world. He was esteemed by Jews and non-Jews alike, not only as a successful Jew, but as a successful citizen. At the same time, he was an active member of the Jewish community. Although he participated widely in civic activities, Robbins' commitment was to Jewish life; he belonged to a country club, a Jewish one; he had many friends, mostly Jewish.

Robbins played gentile to the rest of the Jewish community. By so doing, he attempted to resolve the tensions emerging from the competing behavioral demands exerted by the overlapping stratification systems of the Jewish and the general community. Robbins maintained his ties to the Jewish community by transmitting non-Jewish values to its members. This pattern resulted, of course, in the establishment of commitments to the wider community as well. His claims in this community were, however, not wholly legitimized. Like other Jews, Robbins was excluded from full participation in those associations with gentiles fostering mutual esteem, e.g., membership in gentile country clubs and other non-Jewish social circles. As a result, Robbins' social anchorage lay in the Jewish community. His social role represents a focal point of the underlying conflict between alternative principles of social order, the ethnic community and the general community.

The image of Goldberg was presented not to the wider community, but specifically to the Jewish community. He was eulogized as a person profoundly dedicated to Jewish values. By traditional standards, he was a "good Jew." Nevertheless, he had relatively low status in the Jewish community. He had many close friends, but they were all members of the lower socioeconomic stratum of Jews. The rabbi measured Goldberg's virtue in terms of his allegiance to the basic Jewish institution, the synagogue. In addition to his children's educational attainments, Goldberg was praised for the regularity of his synagogue attendance.

It is clear that Goldberg's basic commitments were to the Jewish community. Whatever tensions he may have experienced were resolved by directing his status activities toward the achievement of Jewish values. Goldberg belonged to no social or civic organizations, nor was he involved in activities requiring acceptance of non-Jewish values. He knew few gentiles and had no gentile friends. When he needed a contact in the wider community for some special purpose, he was likely to go to someone like Robbins, who had the necessary connections rather than to a non-Jew. Goldberg's social role in the Jewish community involved attaining as many Jewish values as possible, or rejecting as many non-Jewish values as possible.

The varying social positions of Robbins and Goldberg illustrate the differential consequences of social change within the North City community. Although both were Rumanian immigrants, Robbins became a wealthy and leading Jew, while Goldberg remained relatively poor. Economic and occupational factors contributed to the disparity in the status situations of these two men. Equally important is the fact that Goldberg chose to retain his early loyalties to Jewish institutions while Robbins chose to transform his original ties. Goldberg's life was rooted in the core of the Jewish community where the status lines between minority and majority communities appear clear-cut. He believed Jews and gentiles should not associate with one another. Robbins, on the other hand, existed on the periphery of the Jewish community where status lines separating it from the wider community are blurred. He believed that Jews should try to associate with gentiles and that gentiles should allow them to do so. Had they known one another, Robbins would no doubt have viewed Goldberg as a "separatist," the epitome of the ghetto Jew. And Goldberg would have regarded Robbins as an "assimilationist," a *goyishe* Jew.

And so North City Jews respond to the status tensions impinging upon their life situations. These tensions are generated by the two opposing poles of their minority situation, the Jewish community and the general community. Jews look to both communities for social approval. North City Jews are, therefore, uncertain about who their status audience is and what social world offers them the best status chances. As a result of the relationship between the stratification system of the Jewish community and that of the general community, those with higher status in the Jewish community have greater access to the non-Jewish world. Clubniks adopt more of the dominant values and interact more with non-Jews than lodgniks. A major consequence of the stratification system of the Jewish community, thus, is to distribute differential access to the values and activities of the dominant society.

THE JEWISH STATUS SYSTEM: THEORETICAL ISSUES

The stratification system of the Jewish community in North City is not a replica in miniature of what exists in the dominant society. Membership in a minority group does make a difference. For all the apparent social distinctions and distance between upper- and lower-strata Jews, they have much in common. Although at two ends of the social hierarchy, they share a past that has helped to mold them. Claims for status are based almost entirely on newly acquired wealth. High-status Jews are not distinguished by early settlement, family lineage, old wealth, or prestigeful occupations. Nor do they have any special religious or cultural background differentiating them from the rest of the minority community. They too are Jews. They do, however, distinguish themselves from low-status Jews by emulating patterns of non-Jewish behavior (or what they regard as non-Jewish), criteria of status that are at best ephemeral for them. They thereby compromise their honor in the eyes of low-status Jews, who charge them with living like *goyim*.

Lacking the institutional support for their superior social position that characterizes the upper stratum of the general society, high-status Jews resort to elaborate patterns of protection against usurpers of status. They have learned from the experience of their own mobility and meet threats to their hard-won status with the tactics of exclusion familiar in the outside world. For example, they too bar "outsiders" from membership in their clubs.

Evident among the upper strata of Jews are patterns of conspicuous consumption encouraging styles of life based on the public display of wealth. Everything that money can buy gets caught up in the intensely invidious struggle to establish the desired status identity. This pattern is by no means peculiar to rich Jews. It reflects the problems faced by all *nouveaux riches* in a society ideologically claiming equality. They must legitimize their status in a social setting that discourages institutionalized status distinctions. Material symbols provide the most readily accessible evidence of status. What you display speaks for who you are.

The difficulties of the *nouveaux riches* are compounded

when they must be resolved within the context of a minority community. For Jews, there are special criteria of status deriving from such Jewish institutions as the synagogue and fund-raising agencies that are independent of the requirements of the general status structure. Characteristically "Jewish" and "non-Jewish" patterns of taste and leisure time must be reckoned with by the Jewish status-seeker. Furthermore, since Jews are concentrated within a limited range of occupations, the relationship between occupation and prestige is not the same as in the general community. Among second-generation Jews, there is little variation in the social standing of their occupations. Even the profitable businesses are not ones that ordinarily rank high in the esteem of the wider community. Income, therefore, becomes the significant differentiating criterion of status.

The social elaboration of variations in income has unexpectedly produced more differentiation within Pinecrest Club than Silverman Lodge. The substrata within the club depend as much on economic affluence as status. The wider range of income has resulted in a variety of values and life styles within the club. Although all clubniks are Jewish, some are more "Jewish" than others. It is immaterial whether the "non-Jewish" clubniks acquired their characteristic style of life before or after joining Pinecrest. What is important is that, once a member, the high-status Jew has greater access to alternative value systems. The options available to the clubnik are beyond the ken of the lodgnik. The clubnik's world is a complex one involving more value choices than the world of the lodgniks.

Lodge members are recruited from strata left behind in the race for economic success, the one means of gaining status open to the minority-group member. Consequently, the lodgnik's status depends upon the observance of traditional Jewish values. Clubniks, willing to adopt non-Jewish values at the cost of their traditional ones, have low status in terms of lodgnik standards. Their high status, however, is guaranteed by their superior class position and access to general values.

The status situation thus has a peculiar complexity. Lodgniks grant clubniks high status on the basis of general non-Jewish criteria and low status on the basis of traditional Jewish criteria. Clubniks are convinced that the status criteria they accept are the norms for the entire Jewish community. As far as they are concerned, lodge membership is a low-status activity not only for them, but for anybody. Membership in the country club or any non-Jewish organization, on the other hand, is deemed prestigeful. Lodgniks are willing to grant the status value of club membership, but since it is beyond the pale of possibility for them, they see no reason even to aspire to it. Clubniks remain the arbiters of status in the Jewish community of North City.

Class and status in the Jewish community do not entirely correspond to class and status in the general community. As the nature of our sample suggests, there are relatively few Jews in North City who are "poor" by general standards. Nor are there many who are "rich" by same standards. (And those who are rich lack the status and power of their gentile peers.) In the Jewish community Pinecrest Club represents the upper class and Silverman Lodge the lower class. In the general community, most Pinecrest members would be upper-middle, and some perhaps lower-upper, class. Silverman members would be middle and lower-middle class. If the two communities were merged, clubniks would lose and lodgniks gain status.

This social merger is not impending. However, a consideration of its hypothetical consequences suggests the major source of tension for high-status Jews. They are not qualified for membership in the upper class of the gentile world. Jewish parvenus would be deprived of the high status the minority group is willing to grant them if they were to be swallowed up by the larger society. They are, therefore, understandably reluctant to sever their remaining ties with the Jewish community. The community, and their special relation to it, is, after all, the precondition of their status.

Claims to status in the general community made by high-status Jews do not necessarily indicate a desire for integration into that community. They are designed to promote status chances among *Jews* who value non-Jewish behavior (i.e., high-status Jews). The low-status Jews are little aware of their status chances in the general community. Their acceptance of traditional Jewish values and institutions ideologically commits them to the separate existence of the Jewish community.

Regardless of the difference in social position of high- and low-status Jews, their activities maintain the internal status system of the minority community. The two strata live differently, but their social relations are mutually oriented. Each stratum accepts the legitimacy of the social position of the other. High-status Jews depend on their low-status fellows to support their relative social superiority by acting as foils in the in-group contests of the status game. In return, low-status Jews expect their wealthy brethren to serves as "ambassadors" to the wider community in order to gain advantage for their "people" (meaning, of course, low-status Jews).

High-status Jews are also role models for the rest of the minority community, whom they educate in previously unknown non-Jewish values. They guarantee their favorable position by monopolizing these values and controlling their availability to less fortunate brothers. The latter, in turn, monopolize traditional Jewish values and, to some extent, control their availability to high-status Jews (as in the case of Hebrew education). In this way, North City Jews are stratified by their differential access to both Jewish and non-Jewish values.

The community is stratified not by one, but several systems. Although second-generation Jews in North City share a common minority situation as well as a commitment to certain values, the findings of this study do not justify the specification of a single set of Jewish status values. On the contrary, the evidence indicates the existence of differences in values and styles of life among Jews associated with status systems that cut across the two sample groups. This social differentiation is particularly true in the case of the country club.

Clubniks have a wider, more varied range of social responses than lodgniks. The analysis of the data uncovered greater homogeneity among lodge members' responses, which are usually concentrated in one or two cells of a given frequency distribution. In contrast, the variety of clubnik responses shows up in split frequency distributions. For example, 96 per cent of the lodgniks and 68 per cent of the clubniks cluster in the income brackets of $3,000 to $5,000 and $20,000 to $50,000 respectively. Seventy-eight per cent of the lodgniks and 44 per cent of the clubniks are concentrated in the occupational categories of proprietor and craftsman and professional and managerial respectively. Most lodgniks live in the North Side and clubniks in the South Side, but the latter are much more dispersed. Similarly, club members engage in a greater variety of social activities and have access to more social circles.

Still, the strata are part of a coherent social system, organized less by value consensus than by underlying institutional configurations such as the synagogue and fund-raising. Jews in North City, regardless of their status, are all subject to the requirements of their institutions. These institutions, no longer traditionally structured, now represent a mixture of Jewish and non-Jewish norms and values. And Jews are stratified according to their relative access to these Jewish and non-Jewish values. Nevertheless, social stratification is structurally linked to institutions, which are a critical source of values. Rather than a causal force, value consensus, or lack of it, is thus a product of the relationship between social stratification and institutions. Social strata are regulated by institutional norms, as well as by the requirements of the stratification system. Values (usually social goals) may therefore become ideologies defending or rejecting the institutions of a community or status claims made within them. In this way, the minority situation is defined by the existing institutional arrangements of both the minority community and the dominant society.

ENTER: THE THIRD GENERATION

This then is the social world into which the third generation is born—a highly stratified world organized around a common minority situation. It is a world full of paradoxes now a source of conflict for the younger generation. The second generation is economically secure, but uncertain of its social status. Members of the older generation employ material criteria of evaluation, but also look with favor upon patterns of behavior based on nonmaterial values. Secular education is prized, but as a means to an occupational end. They are Jews suspicious of gentiles, but eager for their social approval. Religious observance is minimal, but religious identity is not rejected. Association is still based upon Jewish birth rather than shared interests.

Above all, the second generation wants to pass on to its children an acculturated world that is both secular and secure. The fathers toil so that their children may enjoy the fruits of their labor. The heritage of the third generation, however, is not an unmixed blessing. Along with the comforts of financial security come the tensions of a new status. How does the third generation respond to the world of its fathers?

Part Three

CONFLICTS OF THE THIRD GENERATION

6
The Welcome Heritage

THE TENSIONS EXPERIENCED by second-generation Jews are derived in part from the conflicts inherent in the structure of a minority community. They have responded in the only ways they could, jealously guarding the community they brought forth under social duress against both internal and external threat. Although this generation has paved the way for greater access to the values of the dominant society, its own achievement rests on economic rather than social advances. Deprived of the rewards of social acceptance in the larger community, the second generation invests its hopes in its children, grooming them for a life outside the pale of the gilded ghetto.

The ethnic community, sheltering the second generation from the pain of rebuff, challenges its young heirs to formulate new social perspectives. Part of the heritage of the third generation is minority-group membership in a world it never made, a changing world in which yesterday's resolutions are the source of today's conflicts. With the maturing of the third generation there emerges a new style of life different from those of the past, one that embodies tensions created by the very achievements of earlier generations. The nature and extent of the social change between the generations can be determined by a comparison of characteristic economic, religious, and social behavior of third-generation sons with that of their second-generation fathers. The main proposition guiding this investigation states that a generation arrives at some resolution of the shared tensions of its life situation in terms of its available means and common conditions. For the third generation, the following theoretical expectations are suggested:

I. The economic resolutions of the second generation tend to be accepted with modification by the third generation, i.e.:
A. If there is a successful family business, then the son is likely to enter it.
B. If there is no family business, then the son tends to enter such traditionally non-Jewish occupations as the salaried professions.

II. The religious resolutions of the second generation tend to be accepted by the third generation, i.e.:
A. In so far as the religious institutions of the second generation are adapted to the values of the dominant society, they are adopted by members of the third generation.
B. The participation of the third generation in religious institutions varies with type of occupation.
1. If members of the third generation are in traditionally ethnic occupations, then they are more likely to be associated with the religiously based institutions of the established Jewish community.
2. If members of the third generation enter the higher-status occupations of the general society, then they are less likely to be associated with the religiously based institutions of the established Jewish community.

III. The social resolutions of the second generation tend to be rejected by the third generation i.e.:

A. In so far as third-generation Jews strive to minimize the invidious social consequences of minority-group membership, they experience tensions in the realm of status as a result of closer association with non-Jews.

B. The social principles underlying the resolution of tensions are based on status rather than ethnic birth.

The changes predicted from second to third generation are summarized in Table 19 which restates the hypotheses to be tested as theoretically expected differences between the two generations. Fewest changes are predicted in religious patterns of behavior, more in economic patterns, and still more in social behavior.

THE SAMPLE

The student of generations faces certain theoretical problems in defining his categories. To define the third generation of American Jews, for instance, as the native-born children of native-born parents might well be misleading and sociologically inaccurate. Prior research has established that younger immigrants are Americanized relatively rapidly and soon resemble their native-born age mates in the second generation. This is especially true of those immigrants who have at least some of their schooling and their first work experiences here. These experiences, combined with their flexibility and adaptability, hasten the Americanization of young immigrants, and their children then are third generation in the social meaning of the concept, if not in the more limited chronological meaning. As a critical variable in the formation of behavior patterns and attitudes, age circumscribes the delineation of any generation. Included in the third generation for our study are those whose fathers ar-

TABLE 19. Predicted Differences between Second
and Third Generations

I. The third generation accepts the more successful *economic resolutions* of the second generation and improves upon the less satisfactory ones.

VARIABLE	GENERATION IN WHICH ATTRIBUTE OCCURS WITH GREATEST FREQUENCY *
1. Occupations in trade, commerce, manufacturing	Second
2. Occupations of high prestige level	Third
3. Salaried employment	Third
4. High educational level	Third
5. High income level	Second

II. The third generation accepts the *religious resolutions* of the second generation.

VARIABLE	GENERATION IN WHICH ATTRIBUTE OCCURS WITH GREATEST FREQUENCY
1. Synagogue membership	Both
2. Conservative or Reform	Both
3. Synagogue attendance	Both
4. Observance of religious ritual	Both
5. Speak Yiddish	Second

III. The third generation rejects the *social resolutions* of the second generation.

VARIABLE	GENERATION IN WHICH ATTRIBUTE OCCURS WITH GREATEST FREQUENCY
1. Live on North Side	Second
2. Jewish neighborhood	Second
3. Only Jewish friends	Second
4. Only Jewish organizations	Second

* This table summarizes the theoretical expectancies under ideal conditions. In reality, all the members of one generation are not characterized by a particular attribute which all the members of the other lack. Empirically, significantly more members of one generation than the other will have a given attribute.

rived in the United States before they were 18, as well as
those whose parents were born in this country.[1]

Defining the members of the third generation is one thing,
finding them another. Rabbis of congregations and presi-
dents of Jewish organizations popular among young married
couples were contacted. Perusal of their membership lists
yielded the names of those most likely to be third generation.
The theoretical drawback of this process is obvious; the
use of such membership lists introduces a bias in the direction
of Jewish affiliation, a bias less serious than it may appear,
however. Synagogue and organization members themselves
represent degrees of commitment to Jewish institutions;
some join synagogues only to send their children to Sunday
School, rarely attending services more than once a year, if
that; others join B'nai B'rith in order to bowl once a week,
usually neglecting business meetings.

The review of the historical setting of the North City
Jewish community suggests that any sample drawn from it
may be limited by a disproportionate representation of affiliated Jews. This need not invalidate any research based on
such a sample; knowledge of the social context of the sample
controls the inferences permitted by the data. Still, it is true
that it is the unaffiliated Jew who is of equal, if not more,
sociological interest. One way to locate the unaffiliated is
through informal friendships. Men may withdraw from active participation in the community, yet still retain Jewish
friends.

Informants and respondents were asked for the names of
third-generation Jews who do not belong to synagogues or
Jewish organizations. A sample of 100 respondents was

1. Other students have followed this practice in defining generations for purposes of sociological study. See W. Lloyd Warner
and Leo Srole, *The Social Systems of American Ethnic Groups*
(New Haven, Yale University Press, 1945).

drawn randomly from all the available names.[2] This sample, providing data on both fathers and sons, is a different one from the selected sample used to study the stratification of the Jewish community; the third-generation sample encompasses the full range of classes within the community rather than two contrasting status groups. No claim is made, however, about the "representativeness" of the sample. Respondents were located in the only way possible at this point, and the resulting sample is adequate for isolating the characteristic patterns of behavior of the third generation. (The frequency, however, with which various patterns occur in the total population cannot be measured reliably.)

Inevitably there are some included in the sample who are not third generation. Thirty-five per cent of the respondents are literally third generation, i.e., their fathers were born in the United States. Another 49 per cent have fathers who came to the United States before the age of 18, making their sons third generation by sociological definition. The 16 per cent whose fathers came after they were 18 represent a very useful error in sampling. Since the interest of this study is in sociological age mates, these 16 second-generation Jews provide control data for comparing the consequences of sociological age grading with those of chronological generation.

The majority of the respondents are Eastern European in origin, and all but two of the 65 fathers who were not born in the United States arrived before 1926. Sixty-nine per cent were born in the North City area and 82 per cent are

2. Men, rather than women, were selected because of our interest in the social consequences of occupational status. Data on economic, religious, and social behavior were obtained in personal interviews with respondents, who provided information on both themselves and their fathers, in so far as it was possible. (Most respondents had no difficulty in answering questions about their fathers' observable patterns of behavior.)

married. Eighty-five per cent of the sample are under 35 years of age, the mean age being 29.8 years; very few are over 40.

In the interest of accuracy, the analysis that follows is based only on the 84 respondents who are third generation. It should be noted, however, that there are *no* significant differences in social characteristics and patterns of behavior between members of the third generation and their second-generation age mates. The shared social experiences of age peers are more critical in determining behavior than membership in the abstract category of generation of American nativity. The age group thus appears to have more explanatory power for social behavior than the nativity group. The control data provided by our 16 second-generation young Jews, therefore, permits the rejection of chronological generation as an explanation of characteristic third-generation traits in favor of sociological generation.

The social characteristics dealt with in this chapter are economic and religious. The extent to which the third generation accepts the cultural heritage of its fathers in these institutional spheres is suggested by the theoretical framework.

Economic Conflict Resolutions

The third generation does more than accept the economic resolutions of its fathers; it improves them. (See Table 20 for a summary of the significance of the observed relationships between generation and economic characteristics.) The third generation has attained a higher occupational status than the second. (See Table 21.) Almost four times as many sons as fathers are in the professions and semi-professions, but only one-third as many sons are in craft and service occupations. Although the same proportion of both fathers and sons are in clerical and sales work, sig-

TABLE 20. Economic Resolutions of Second
and Third Generations

VARIABLE	SECOND GENERATION *Per Cent*	THIRD GENERATION *Per Cent*	SIGNIFICANCE OF ASSOCIATION WITH GENERATION
Trade, commerce, or manufacturing	51.2	30.9	Significant
Professional and semi-professional	11.9	46.5	Significant
Salaried employment	27.4	54.8	Significant
College education or more	20.3	88.2	Significant
Income over $10,000 a year	51.6	33.3	Significant

nificantly fewer sons are in some aspect of trade, commerce, or manufacturing.

Almost all of the members of the third generation who are in business are in their fathers' businesses. Only a few are themselves small independent proprietors. As expected, in those cases where the fathers have achieved economic

TABLE 21. Occupations of Second and Third Generations

OCCUPATION	FATHERS *Number*	*Per Cent*	SONS *Number*	*Per Cent*
Retail proprietor or executive	22	26.2	11	13.1
Manager or executive *	21	25.0	15	17.8
Professional or semi-professional	10	11.9	39	46.5
Clerical or sales	13	15.5	13	15.5
Craft, service, foreman, peddler	18	21.4	6	7.1
Total	84	100.0	84	100.0

Significant: 4 d.f.   chi-square = 27.83 $P < .001$ $T = .287$

* Wholesale distribution, light manufacturing, salvage, transportation, trade, commerce. All but two of the sons in this occupational category are in their fathers' businesses.

mobility, the sons are accepting their successful economic resolutions. Those young men who do not have family businesses to enter (or professional practices to take over) improve their occupational status by entering both the independent and the salaried professions and semi-professions. These professions have higher and more general status in the community than the businesses characteristic of the second generation (although the latter may be highly profitable).[3]

To test the relationship between the economic resolutions of the two generations, father's occupation is cross-tabulated with son's occupation. Sixty-three per cent of those whose fathers are successful businessmen or independent professionals are also in business (their fathers') or the independent professions. Only 21 per cent of those whose fathers are not as successful are now in family businesses or professions. On the other hand, 42 per cent of the latter, rejecting the unsatisfactory economic resolutions of their fathers, enter new and traditionally non-Jewish occupations such as the salaried professions. (See Table 22.)

A similar relationship is observed when son's occupation is cross-tabulated with father's income. Fifty-seven per cent of the sons whose fathers earn over $10,000 a year go into their fathers' businesses or the independent professions. Only 27 per cent of those whose fathers earn less than $10,000 do so. The latter tend to enter the new occupations. (See Table 23.)

These cross-tabulations provide evidence of who is ac-

3. Among the professions and semi-professions are included medicine, law, university teaching, engineering, scientific research, journalism, public relations. Characteristic traditional businesses include light manufacturing (e.g., garment manufacturing), salvage, auto distribution, retail stores. The occupational classification used follows that of the U.S. Census.

TABLE 22. Father's Occupation and Son's Occupation

SON'S OCCUPATION	FATHER'S OCCUPATION			
	SELF-EMPLOYED BUSINESSMAN OR INDEPENDENT PROFESSIONAL		OTHER	
	Number	Per Cent	Number	Per Cent
Father's business or independent professional	32	62.7	7	21.2
Self-employed business or lower-status occupation	12	23.5	12	36.4
Non-Jewish occupation	7	13.8	14	42.4
Total	51	100.0	33	100.0

Significant: 2 d.f.   chi-square = 15.06   P < .001   T = .356

cepting their fathers' economic resolutions and help to explain why the highly significant occupational differences between the generations are only moderately associated with generation membership alone. Many of the third generation are making occupational advances over the second, but others are retaining their fathers' already established positions. Variables of both class background and generation are significant determinants of the occupational distribution of the third generation.

TABLE 23. Father's Income and Son's Occupation

SON'S OCCUPATION	FATHER'S INCOME			
	UNDER $10,000		OVER $10,000	
	Number	Per Cent	Number	Per Cent
Father's business or independent profession	8	26.7	31	57.4
Self-employed business or lower-status occupation	9	30.0	15	27.8
Non-Jewish occupation	13	43.3	8	14.8
Total	30	100.0	54	100.0

Significant: 2 d.f.   chi-square = 10.19   P < .01   T = .293

The successful family business has all the virtues of the well-beaten path. It offers maximum security and assurance of executive position to the son and heir.

> I'd just as soon take it easy and let things go along. I chose my father's business (wholesale distribution) as the line of least resistance.

> Being Jewish doesn't help you when you want to advance as a metallurgist in industry so I gave up my salaried job to take over my father's scrap iron business.[4]

Not all of the second-generation businesses are equally attractive to the sons. The small retail store affording a hard-earned and precarious income is rarely accepted as a suitable means of livelihood by the son. Those who reject the marginal economic resolutions of their fathers explain themselves in this way:

> I didn't want to spend eighteen hours a day as a pharmacist building up a drug store. I hated my father's store. I decided to do what I want despite what others say. I won't scramble for money all the time.

The acceptance of the second generation's economic resolutions is highly selective. Only the more successful resolutions are adopted, and these are resolutions that are not uniquely Jewish.

Where there is no such family business, members of the third generation seek status in the new and traditionally

4. Verbatim reports of statements made by respondents are used to provide qualitative documentation. They are useful in interpreting the quantitative data and illuminate their meaning either by characterizing the typical attitudes or by presenting the more extreme negative or positive reactions. These statements are not sufficient basis for generalization, but they do provide insight into the nature of the conflict resolutions of the third generation.

non-Jewish occupations. Although they reject the particular economic resolutions of their fathers, they accept the value the second generation places on economic mobility. Although one respondent complained,

> I was forced into a profession to get anywhere since I had no family business to fall back on,

many others enjoyed the advantage of greater freedom of occupational choice. One respondent described a characteristic occupational decision:

> I discovered I had a flair for selling, writing, and drawing, and advertising seemed lucrative. I was free to choose what I wanted, unlike most of my friends, since my father (a reporter) had no business to pass on.

The son without a business to inherit chooses from an increasingly wider range of occupations. Occupations such as advertising which are relatively new and in need of trained personnel have not yet had an opportunity to establish restrictive employment practices. Consequently, they are particularly attractive to young Jews.

Even among the professions, third-generation Jews are beginning to enter the newer, salaried ones. Eighty per cent of the professionals among the fathers are independent professionals practicing law, medicine, and dentistry. In contrast, 36 per cent of the professional sons are in such salaried professions as engineering, teaching, research, and another 20 per cent are in semi-professions such as journalism, advertising, and public relations.

Lacking the windfall of a family business, many young Jews must seek employment elsewhere. A greater number of sons than fathers are found in salaried employment; fifty-five per cent of the sons are in the salaried employ of others in contrast to only half as many of the fathers. (See

Table 24.) There is more than a numerical difference in the salaried employment of the two generations. The qualitative differences in the nature of the employment are also significant. The fathers are employed as skilled craftsmen, the sons as highly trained professionals and semi-professionals.

TABLE 24. Self-Employment and Salaried Employment of Second and Third Generations

EMPLOYMENT STATUS	FATHERS		SONS	
	Number	*Per Cent*	*Number*	*Per Cent*
Self-employed (or in father's business)	61	72.6	38	45.2
Salaried employment	23	27.4	46	54.8
Total	84	100.0	84	100.0

Significant: 1 d.f.   chi-square = 13.01   P < .001   phi = .333
(c = o) *

* c refers to the cell that we theoretically expect to be o when the fourfold table is set up as follows: $\frac{a \quad b}{c \quad d}$. Phi square then is the measure of the degree to which the logical model is approximated by the data.

The fathers are self-employed as businessmen (most of them small businessmen). Few of the sons are literally self-employed as yet. Those who are in their fathers' businesses, however, are potentially self-employed and classified as such for purposes of study, although they remain on an executive's salary as long as their fathers continue to run the businesses. Similarly, young independent professionals (such as lawyers) still in the early stages of their careers may be in the employ of established professional firms now, but are aiming for self-employment in the near future.

Members of the second generation made every effort to be self-employed if it was at all possible. They were usually unable to find employment with gentiles. (The few who were so employed had cause to be anxious about the security of this employment.) When they did work for others, it was for other Jews. The third generation finds more employment opportunities open to them, even with non-Jewish firms. An increasing proportion of them equip themselves with specialized training, and the industrial need for their skills outweighs any prior reluctance about hiring Jews. Few members of the second generation even considered, for example, engineering as a career, since employment opportunities were so scarce for Jews before World War II. Now, the Jewish engineer no longer worries about finding—or keeping—a job.

Evidence from other studies throughout the United States suggests that discrimination has declined sufficiently so that young Jews no longer regard independent self-employment as the only guarantee of security. Those of the third generation interested in business increasingly prefer to work for large organizations rather than become retail proprietors. Similarly, the greatest increase in Jewish professionals has been in the salaried intellectual professions traditionally closed to Jews (journalism, architecture, engineering, college teaching).[5] The growing acceptance of salaried employment reflects, in part, the desire of young Jews to live as their non-Jewish peers do. When they choose a nine-to-five job rather than the twelve-hour day of the small retail shopkeeper, they are also choosing a new type of social life, which will be discussed in the next chapter.

The importance of specialized training for breaking into traditionally non-Jewish occupations is apparent in the fact that salaried Jews in business usually work for other Jews, but salaried professionals are just as likely (or more

5. Nathan Glazer, "Social Characteristics of American Jews, 1654–1954," 3–43.

likely) to be working for non-Jewish firms—a relatively recent development in employment conditions.[6]

Education is the passport into the gentile world, and an increasing number of young Jews are acquiring an increasing amount of it. None of the sons ended his education with grade school as almost half of the fathers did. (See Table 25.) (These are fathers who came from Europe as children with only *cheder* education, i.e., primary schooling in religious learning.) Eighty-eight per cent of the sons have had some college education or more; 29 per cent

TABLE 25. Educational Levels of Second and Third Generations

EDUCATIONAL LEVEL	FATHERS		SONS	
	Number	*Per Cent*	*Number*	*Per Cent*
Cheder or grade school	40	47.6	0	0.0
High school, technical, or business school	27	32.1	10	11.8
Some college	5	5.9	21	25.0
Completed college	6	7.2	24	28.6
Graduate or professional school	6	7.2	29	34.6
Total	84	100.0	84	100.0

Significant: 4 d.f.   chi-square = 83.57   P < .001   T = .499

completed college and another 36 per cent have had graduate or professional schooling. Three-quarters of them received their degrees from the local university. Only 20 per cent of the fathers went to college, and most of these are fathers born in the United States. The wives of the respondents are also highly educated. Although fewer

6. Eighty-eight per cent of those respondents employed in business work for Jewish firms, whereas only 22 per cent of those employed in the professions do so. The majority of these professionals are specialists, rather than general practitioners.

wives than husbands have had graduate or professional training, as many have gone to college.

Advanced education is the necessary prerequisite for the new professions. What these educational and occupational advances mean financially for the third generation is difficult to determine at this point. The incomes of the third generation are significantly lower than those of the second. (See Table 26.) The average annual income of

TABLE 26. Annual Gross Incomes of Second and Third Generations

INCOME	FATHERS		SONS	
	Number	Per Cent	Number	Per Cent
Under $5,000	7	11.3	13	15.5
$5,000–9,999	23	37.1	43	51.2
$10,000–19,999	17	27.4	21	25.0
Over $20,000	15	24.2	7	8.3
Total	62*	100.0	84	100.0

Significant: 3 d.f. chi-square = 8.07 P < .05 T = .178

* 26.2 per cent of the sons did not know their fathers' incomes (often because the father was retired or deceased).

the fathers (i.e., those whose incomes were known to the sons) is $14,314, for the sons $10,291. Proportionately, three times as many fathers as sons have incomes over $20,000 a year.[7]

These differences, while significant, are not great and occur mostly at the upper brackets of the income range. The most likely explanation of the disparity in income is the difference in age between fathers and sons. The fathers

7. Interestingly enough, the younger sons with incomes in the upper brackets (usually in their fathers' businesses) are more reluctant to state their incomes. They are somewhat defensive in reporting (and sometimes explaining) a high income they are not convinced they are "earning." Young professionals, on the other hand, willingly give the details of their limited financial resources.

are already well established in their occupations and their incomes are stable. Most of the sons are still in the early stages of their careers with moderate incomes increasing every year. Even those in their fathers' businesses, the young married country club set, are at present on salaries appropriate to their age and relatively limited experience.

A cross-tabulation of age and income within the third generation suggests that income does increase with age. Twenty-four per cent of respondents under 35 years of age earn over $10,000 a year in contrast to the 71 per cent of those over 35 who do so. Most of the younger members of the third generation earn less than $10,000 a year, but can expect to be earning more by the time they are 35. It remains to be seen, however, whether or not the future income level of the sons will reach that of their fathers. Many of the sons are in professions where their potential earning power is considerably higher than their present income, but not necessarily as high as that of successful second-generation businessmen. But the third generation is at least as concerned with the general status of its chosen occupations as with the income.[8]

The mien of the third generation is one of general contentment with its economic position. Few feel economically deprived in any way. More than half have fulfilled their occupational aspirations; another 19 per cent had no particular aspirations. Of the remaining 30 per cent most had changed their occupational plans because they found that a particular occupation was not sufficiently remunerative, or that it was too difficult a field to break into and get ahead. Only a few specifically cite being Jewish as a reason for changing their occupational plans, i.e., they decided not

8. Even those sons who eventually enter such profitable family businesses as salvage, plumbing supplies, or garment manufacturing often first acquire independent status as metallurgists, sanitary engineers, or bachelors of business administration in textiles.

to become a professor of philosophy or an engineer because "at the time" it was almost impossible for a Jew to get a job in these fields, or so they were advised. Those most likely to have unfulfilled dreams of glory are the older members of the third generation who encountered more discrimination before World War II than their juniors do now. They acknowledge that "things have changed now."

Further indication of the self-satisfaction of third-generation Jews is found in their plans for the future. One third want to continue in much the same way. Most of the rest want either to advance in their careers, to establish themselves independently in their professions, or to take over the family business. Less than 5 per cent want to start their own businesses or seek new opportunities, although several fancy themselves as "independent entrepreneurs" in the near future dabbling in investments and real estate—with money accumulated in their fathers' businesses, of course. All in all, economically speaking, this is the best of all possible worlds.

The economic euphoria of the third generation colors many of its attitudes. Fifty-six per cent, for example, feel no urge to strive for economic "success." They prefer rather "to do what they want," to have jobs they enjoy, and to have sufficient time left over to spend with their families. These contented ones are not searching for an elusive "pot of gold," nor are they cultivating any ulcers. A number of respondents contrast their own philosophy of material gain with that of their fathers. Interesting changes are taking place in this area, changes in conformity with recent transformations in American ideology. The third generation may achieve occupational status, but its motivation for attaining the once compelling dream of "success" is less strong than that of the second generation. Young Jews refuse to consecrate themselves to economic pursuits.

I don't feel as dedicated to the business (salvage) as my father. Sure I want money, but I don't want to work as hard for it as my father did. For instance, I hate to have to go on business trips and leave my family, but my father loves it. His life is his business and he's entirely wrapped up in it.

My father's generation may have felt pressure to achieve success, but this generation is lazier.

In my background, it was important to get money. My family grubbed for it all the time. I rebelled against just working, eating, and sleeping. I thought there must be other important things in life, like what you do with money. I didn't want to spend my life working at something I hated (drug store). Money, after all, is not as important as what you do with it.

Several observers of the Jewish scene have suggested that aspirations have changed from second to third generation. The fathers had the ambition to build successful businesses and professional practices, the sons only the ambition to inherit them. In wanting to be like everyone else, the third-generation Jew wants also to feel that he doesn't have to strive unduly for success. He prefers to believe that he doesn't have to prove anything to anybody by earning an ever increasing income, and he is wary of offending his well-adjusted neighbors by any display of aggressive ambition. Like everyone else he knows, he wants comfort and security for himself and his family, and time in which to enjoy the income he does earn. He concentrates on spending his money and finding out what it can do for him rather than on enlarging his income. This permits him to avoid incurring the hostility of his non-Jewish peers.

The decline of economic tensions in the third generation

offers evidence that many of the economic problems of the minority situation were solved effectively by the second generation. In large part, however, the lowered economic sights simply reflect the broader changes in goals among the younger generation of all Americans. Brogan observes a general reassessment of values among Americans. "One [new type of value decision] is the decision for leisure rather than for ever-expanding income. The man continually striving loses the chance for leisure. His very recreations are driven by a passion to 'succeed.' "[9] Taking for granted the advantages an older generation struggled to acquire is hardly unique to young Jews.[10] "Few self-made men can resist the temptation to give their sons 'advantages' that they didn't have and these advantages often include an education that alienates the son from his father's simple world."[11] Young Jews and non-Jews alike want the comforts of life without having to pay the high price of overwork. They assume they will come into possession of these comforts as a result of a job they will have no difficulty in obtaining (especially if it's in a family business).[12]

Although the values of the third generation are certainly part of a general climate of opinion favoring "peace of mind" over "success," they also reflect changes taking

9. D. W. Brogan, "Unnoticed Changes in America," *Harper's Magazine*, February 1957, 33.

10. See John Seeley, R. Alexander Sim, Elizabeth Looseley, *Crestwood Heights: A Study of the Culture of Suburban Life* (New York, Basic Books, 1956), pp. 119, 130–1 for indication of change from strong career strivings in one generation to a desire for continued material comfort in the next.

11. Brogan, "Unnoticed Changes," 33.

12. Philip E. Jacob's 15-year study of college students concludes that, "A dominant characteristic of the current student generation is that they are *gloriously contented* both in regard to the present day-to-day activity and their outlook for the future." Quoted in Terry Ferrer, "Our Egocentric College Youth," *Saturday Review*, September 14, 1957, 19.

place within the Jewish community. Kurt Lewin argued that it was the tensions of marginality characteristic of second-generation Jews which served to generate their intense strivings for success; a decline in such tensions produces diminished ambition. The tensions of the third generation have been eased in important ways.

The men of the third generation are, after all, not "marginal men." Because of their acceptable middle-class American background with its mild version of Judaism, they do not experience their Jewishness as a source of much conflict. Since in many respects they feel more accepted by non-Jews than their fathers, they have little cause for self-hatred or embittered striving for membership in the non-Jewish world. With the problems of survival and success solved by earlier generations, the third generation rarely experiences the degree of tension necessary for the ambition of its fathers. Even Marjorie Morningstar could not fail to take note of the new Philistine of her generation, the young Jew who "wants to be a writer or a forest ranger or a composer or anything except what his father is, because he's ashamed of his father being a Jew, or because he thinks he's too sensitive for business or law, or whatever the damned Freudian reason may be—and he winds up in his father's business just the same. . . ." [13]

What members of the younger generation are concerned with is the cultivation of appropriate styles of life. Education has helped to nurture their interest in this area. Even more than money, they want time to consume and to engage in the proper leisure-time activities. "Today's heroes don't lust for big riches, but they are positively greedy for the good life." [14] The consummate dedication

13. Herman Wouk, *Marjorie Morningstar* (Garden City, N.Y., Doubleday, 1955), pp. 173-4.
14. William H. Whyte, Jr., *The Organization Man* (New York, Simon and Schuster, 1956), p. 250.

of the second generation to business left little time for dabbling in status symbols. The third generation wants to "enjoy life" in a way its fathers did not.

> I won't kill myself for a buck. There's more to living than just money. I'm more concerned with the way I want to live.

> I like my way of life now. I won't cut out activities I like just to earn another buck.

> I want to take it easy and spend time with my family. I make enough to get along—I don't want more money—and the heart attack that goes with it.

> I don't know what the goal would be for making more money. . . . There's no goal in just making money. You only know what your goals are when you're doing what you want.

These are the voices of men whose fathers devoted twelve hours a day to work and the other twelve to worry. Their sons see no point in having money you can't enjoy, and they reject the "materialistic" preoccupation of the fathers. They take for granted, however, a "suitable" income and assume they will continue to earn an adequate living. To be concerned with material gain, however, smacks of "money grubbing," a peculiarly Jewish vice in the stereotypes of American society.

Although few are looking for wealth, 39 per cent anticipate increased incomes. Motivation for economic improvement derives from a desire to provide appropriate standards of living for their families.

> I want to provide adequately for my family and have as much as others have in comforts.

> I want more income since I'm not yet up to the standard of living I'd like to achieve.

These ambitions are eminently reasonable for young men starting out in careers whose income potential increases with time. Although they will not "grub for money," they expect to make enough in the near future to afford the style of life they want. Only 5 per cent express some dedication to the pursuit of their professional interests, regardless of the possibilities of success, financial or otherwise.

The secure aura of economic well-being is enhanced by the fact that few have been handicapped by their Jewishness. Fifty-two per cent feel that being Jewish had no influence whatsoever on their occupational choice. Another 43 per cent feel that being Jewish influenced them to enter a profession, to be self-employed or in public service, and/or to strive for achievement (whether intellectual or financial). Influences of this sort are not considered restrictive. On the contrary, it is still desirable to be motivated to enter a profession, even if the source of such motivation is one's "Jewishness." Even those who chose self-employment because they thought Jews couldn't get ahead any other way do not feel impeded by this. They reason as follows:

I want to be self-employed. I didn't go into TV for that reason. It's just part of my family background. We went through the depression and my father always says you're better off with less on your own. I wouldn't take more money to work for someone else.

I wanted to be self-employed because of the problem of anti-Semitism impeding advancement.

Being Jewish led me to be a self-employed professional. As a Jewish employee in North City, I couldn't have advanced very far. Jewish businesses are all family businesses and I had no way of getting into them.

But my uncle had a law firm I was able to join when I was getting started.

North City has had an especially virulent tradition of discriminatory employment which has influenced even members of the younger generation to work for themselves. Nevertheless, they have no cause for complaint. Even in North City, an increasing number of young Jews claim,

I like working for the company. I have security there and I don't feel the need to be self-employed.

Being Jewish is no longer an economic problem to the third generation. Only 17 per cent feel that their religious identity has either restricted their occupational choice, limiting them to fewer and less desirable occupations, or impeded their opportunities for advancement within their chosen fields. Not many of this generation encounter job discrimination; few even apply for positions in local industries reputed to be discriminatory. Some of the older members of the third generation were counselled out of certain fields when they were making their career decisions because of the difficulty of finding employment for Jews.

I didn't go into the scientific field (chemical research) for fear of not being employed in the big industries that do the research. I felt I had to be an independent professional to get ahead and law seemed to permit mobility.

I wanted to be an engineer originally, but I worried about discrimination since Jews are not hired. Even as a self-employed professional, being Jewish affects you since you get mostly Jewish clients and patients.

The salaried professions are increasingly open to Jews as the demand for highly trained personnel grows. But those seeking lower-middle-class white-collar positions without any particular skill or training to offer still run up against discrimination. In this sample, however, there are few men with only high school education. One respondent, looking for a job as an insurance salesman found that,

> Being Jewish makes it difficult when you don't have real training. If you have special training, being Jewish doesn't matter.

It is easier for a Jew to sell his "skills" on the job market than his "personality." Consequently, he has more access to jobs requiring professional training or technical expertise than to jobs involving executive managerial capacities.

The members of the third-generation sample are a highly educated and disproportionately professional group for whom economic discrimination has rarely been a problem. Complacent in their security, few feel they must be self-employed to insure their source of livelihood. Most respondents are convinced that being Jewish will in no way limit their opportunities for advancement or restrict the number of their business contacts or clients. Some even find their religious identity an asset; there are people who, for example, prefer Jewish professionals because "they're better."

Although the third generation has experienced few occupational restrictions as Jews, it does recognize some occupations as "more Jewish" than others. Perhaps as a result of this awareness, members of the sample have steered away from "Jewish" occupations which lack more general status in the community. Most frequently mentioned as typically "Jewish" occupations are the independent professions (e.g., law and medicine) and retail proprietorships. Factory worker and corporation executive positions are the occupations considered "least Jewish," i.e., respondents believe fewer Jews are found in them than in the others.

The "Jewishness" of an occupation affects its standing in the wider community. In 1953, the North City Junior Chamber of Commerce published a list of "One Hundred Young Men Selected by the Committee for North City's Future." The list, composed mostly of businessmen and such professionals as clergymen, professors, lawyers, and doctors, suggests the type of Jew held in general esteem. Seven Jews were among the chosen and none, except the rabbi of a high-ranking Conservative congregation (whose modern Ivy League approach to religion qualifies him as a representative young clergyman), was in an occupation traditionally associated with Jews in North City. Two were symphony musicians in no way connected with the local Jewish community, one a newspaper columnist. The others included a research chemist, a municipal judge, and a president of a long established manufacturing firm. There are richer Jews in the city, but these six were distinguished by their occupations, which are not the characteristically marginal occupations of an ethnic group.

The immigrant and working-class status of the first generation created tensions to which its sons responded with a fierce drive for success. The second generation was more likely to advance in class than status, but was able to bestow upon its sons all the advantages of economic security, including a college education. The third generation receives its comfortable heritage with some reservations. Although members of this generation have no conscientious objection to the profit they derive from the economic gains of their fathers, they are critical of the "materialistic" values of the older generation. They permit themselves the illusion that interest in money is a peculiar monopoly of Jews, of which they want no part (except in dollars and cents).

The achievement of the second generation brought with it problems requiring resolution by the next generation. The literary voice of the younger generation asks petulantly whether "upper-middle-class Jewish life is different and worse than upper-middle-class life in general" or just different.[15] Heroines of recent Jewish novels insist upon falling in love with unsuitable young men who represent a different way of life from that of their fathers—a way of life that precludes financial success. Young Jews are less concerned with the accumulation of wealth than with the cultivation of appropriate styles of life. Many a bewildered second-generation father has wondered why, if his college educated son is so smart, he isn't rich.

The "materialistic" values and the marginal nature of the occupations [16] of the second generation are a source of tension for its sons. Yet despite any qualms they may have about making money, those of the third generation who are heir to successful family businesses rarely refuse them. They appease an occasionally troublesome conscience by spending their money in different and less "Jewish" ways than their fathers. Those without the "burden" of a family business use advanced education as a key to open the doors of a variety of new occupations. Entry into these occupations is one of the important tension resolutions of the third generation, whose life situation is, in part, a response to the demands of a national economy for increasing levels of expertness among its citizens.

Not all members of the third generation have either

15. Granville Hicks, "Literary Horizons," *Saturday Review*, May 17, 1958, p. 16. For examples, see Herman Wouk, *Marjorie Morningstar*, or Brian Glanville, *The Bankrupts*.

16. Even the garment industry is derogated as the *shmata* (or rag) trade.

the means of access to these new occupations or the motivation. The family business still represents greater security and ease. Nevertheless, these new occupations furnish an escape from social uniqueness for a growing number of young Jews. The occupations are not identifiable as "Jewish" and their status in the general community is high. The impetus for the occupational redistribution of the third generation derives, in part, from the characteristic discrepancy between class and status in the second generation. Entrance into traditionally non-Jewish occupations thus by-passes the tensions inherent in marginal occupations, which are low in status, however profitable they may be.

In sum, we find that members of the third generation have not merely accepted the more successful economic resolutions of their fathers, they have improved upon them. They have achieved considerable occupational mobility and are well satisfied with themselves. Being Jewish has rarely hindered the attainment of their occupational goals, although they are aware of the economic discrimination practiced in North City. They are excluded from the local executive world of "organization men," but they have entered through the back door as salaried professionals and technical experts.

It is quite clear then that the third generation accepts the economic world of its fathers, at least in so far as it is a comfortable world. Here there is no wholesale overthrowing of the goals of the second generation, although accumulation of wealth is exchanged for time to spend it. One generation earns the money, and the next learns how to spend it appropriately. The economic mobility begun by the second generation is extended by its sons, who make their gains in occupational status.

Religious Conflict Resolutions

Theoretically the third generation is expected to accept
the religious resolutions of its fathers, with some modification in the direction of increasing adaptation to the religious patterns of the majority community. In so far as
the religious behavior of the second generation is already
adapted to American life, the hypotheses predict no
differences between the religious behavior of the fathers
and that of the sons. The summary of the differences in
the religious resolutions of the two generations in Table
27 indicates that while this is generally true, a few significant differences do occur.

TABLE 27. Religious Resolutions of Second
and Third Generations

VARIABLE	SECOND GENERATION *Per Cent*	THIRD GENERATION *Per Cent*	SIGNIFICANCE OF ASSOCI- ATION WITH GENERATION
Members of synagogue	91.7	89.3	Not significant
Members of Orthodox synagogues	20.2	1.2	Significant
Attend synagogue on High Holidays and occasionally	69.1	66.7	Not significant
Minimum ritual observance	38.1	41.7	Not significant
Speak Yiddish	84.5	2.4	Significant

The overwhelming majority of both generations belong
to a synagogue (or plan to join in the near future). (See
Table 28.) Among those classified as affiliated sons are included a number who intend to join a synagogue within
the next few years. These are classified as synagogue members, at least in intention, since they continue to attend
services with their parents. They plan to join a synagogue
when they have children of their own. Synagogue affilia-

TABLE 28. Synagogue Affiliation of Second
and Third Generations

SYNAGOGUE AFFILIATION	FATHERS		SONS	
	Number	*Per Cent*	*Number*	*Per Cent*
Belong (or will belong) to synagogue	77	91.7	75	89.3
Do not belong to synagogue	7	8.3	9	10.7
Total	84	100.0	84	100.0

Not Significant: 1 d.f.   chi-square = .276   P > .05

tion is a prerequisite for "responsible parenthood"; it provides the religious education for the young now considered vital to "adjustment."

Suburban life encourages religious affiliation in a generation inclined to regard religion as a good thing both for the individual and the community. "There is a marked tendency to regard religion as a good because it is useful in furthering other major values—in other words, to reverse the ends-means relation implied in the conception of religion as an ultimate value." [17] In accord with the general climate of opinion, Judaism has also become a commodity serving both the psyche of the individual Jew and the survival of the Jewish community. Its social function has particular importance in the suburbs where young Jews, now living with non-Jewish peers, are increasingly conscious of themselves as Jews.[18]

The gilded ghetto permitted their fathers to be irreligious while still enjoying a Jewish social life, but the suburban sons have become a "captive audience" for religious institutions. The suburban synagogue organizes the social life of young Jews, reinforcing old ties and maintaining the

17. Robin Williams, Jr., *American Society* (New York, Knopf, 1955), p. 357.
18. Nathan Glazer, *American Judaism*, p. 113.

distance between Jew and non-Jew. The third generation
has less cause than ever to reject established religious institutions in the suburbs, where religious identity is a prerequisite to social acceptance.

The third generation is indeed conforming to social
pressures, suburban and otherwise, when it accepts the
responsibility of religious affiliation. There are those who
argue, however, that this religious acceptance has special
significance. Both Herberg and Warner, for example, claim
that religion has replaced ethnic membership as the context of identification for Americans.[19] Religion provides
a means of perpetuating group differences that does not
threaten the status of a third generation secure enough to
accept its heritage.

Among those of the third generation who now belong
to a synagogue are many who joined only to send their
children to Sunday School. They are little interested in
organized religious life, but they cannot make use of the
Sunday School without synagogue membership and they
are anxious to raise their offspring as Jews. They are tied
to the synagogue by their desire for religious continuity,
but they would like to see it modernized. They argue, like
their fathers before them, that "much of it is outmoded
and should be changed," but they maintain their affiliation.
However child-centered this orientation toward religious
institutions may be, it involves the third generation in at
least nominal religious participation. The family that wishes
to pass on a religious tradition to its heirs now requires the
assistance of the established institutions of the Jewish community.

Those who remain unaffiliated are a far cry from the
militant rebels of the second generation. Most of them

19. Will Herberg, *Protestant-Catholic-Jew: An Essay in American Religious Sociology* (New York, Doubleday, 1956), pp. 20,
55.

are simply disinterested, or uninterested as yet because they do not need the synagogue to indoctrinate the next generation. The religiously indifferent anticipate the likelihood of joining a synagogue when community and family pressures come to bear on them. They recognize the convenient expediency of synagogue membership.

> I will probably succumb to social pressures and join the Reform Temple since a doctor ought to belong and be seen in synagogue by his patients. Besides, it's a source of contacts.

Few are so negative toward religious institutions as the atypical respondent who argues,

> There's nothing to be gained from synagogue affiliation. I can do a better job with Jewish education for my children on my own. I don't want them to observe ritual and attend synagogue in a formal, meaningless way.

The majority have a tolerant—and even favorable—attitude toward religion. One respondent sums it up with,

> Judaism has changed. . . . Nowadays people enjoy religion and going to synagogue. Rabbis have changed their methods. They're more modern now.

Of those who do belong to a synagogue, only one belongs to an Orthodox congregation, and he intends to switch to a new suburban Conservative one. (None of the unaffiliated ones intend to join an Orthodox synagogue in the future.) More of the second generation are Orthodox; twenty per cent continue to belong to Orthodox synagogues, although another 5 per cent have themselves switched from Orthodox to Conservative or Reform synagogues in recent years. (See Table 29.) This difference

TABLE 29. Denominational Affiliation of Second
and Third Generations

DENOMINATION	FATHERS		SONS	
	Number	Per Cent	Number	Per Cent
Orthodox	17	20.2	1	1.2
Conservative	44	52.4	49	58.3
Reform	16	19.1	14	16.7
None	7	8.3	20 *	23.8
	84	100.0	84	100.0

Significant: 3 d.f. chi-square = 25.19 P < .01 T = .294

* 11 of the sons will join within the next few years.

in Orthodox affiliation between fathers and sons accounts
for the moderate association between generation and denomination, which was not expected. Also accounting for
this association is the proportion of sons as yet unaffiliated
with synagogues independently of their parents' memberships. The unaffiliated 24 per cent is spuriously high, ex-
aggerated by the inclusion of those who intend to join a
synagogue in the near future. It is the continued allegiance
to Orthodoxy of some of the fathers that is the major difference between the generations. Otherwise, the denominational affiliation of the two generations is similar.

It is relevant to note that the sons who do not plan to
join synagogues at all tend to have fathers who are either
Orthodox or nonmembers themselves. The sons of Conservative and Reform fathers belong to, or intend to join,
synagogues, an observation that adds further weight to
the hypothesis predicting the acceptance of second-
generation religious resolutions already adapted to American life.

The majority of sons belong to Conservative synagogues,
and most of the intentions for future membership are
Conservative. Conservatism, a middle-class, "middle-of-the-

road" religion, is appealing to a generation following in its fathers' footsteps. The location of the Conservative synagogues is convenient to the suburbs and their programs of activities are geared to the interests of "young marrieds." The newer Conservative synagogues whose control is not yet vested in the established elements of the community are most likely to attract and actively engage the younger generation. The characteristic reasons for joining the Conservative synagogue are more social than theological.

> I support the new local synagogue (a Conservative one in West Parricus) because it's the most convenient. It permits you to grow with the synagogue and be active since it's not controlled by the older generation. It's really interested in the younger generation.

> I will join the West Parricus synagogue. I can't afford the Reform Temple—it's too expensive. The West Parricus synagogue is more in our age group and in line with what we can afford. But I'm only joining for the sake of the kids so they can go to Sunday School.

The Reform Temple has not picked up many new members from the third generation, other than those whose families already belong. Temple membership is considered expensive for the young married budget and the congregation identified with the more established and successful members of the older generation. Descendants of Eastern Europeans continue to regard Reform Judaism as "too extreme" in spite of its increasing adoption of traditional ritual.

Sixty-five per cent of the sons give as their reason for choosing the synagogue they did join (or will choose when they do join) the fact that their families belong to them.

Only 5 per cent claim that their choice is based upon religious convictions. Another 16 per cent mention such "social" reasons as the friends or contacts they can make within the congregation or the activities provided for their age group. The rest joined in order to be able to send their children to Sunday School. No stronger indication of the third generation's acceptance of the religious institutions of the second can be found than its willingness to join the same synagogue to which the family belongs simply because the family does belong to it. (Some of the synagogues implement this willingness by offering a year's free membership to children of members who are married in the synagogue.)

The majority of both generations (69 per cent of the fathers and 67 per cent of the sons) attend synagogue only on High Holidays or on High Holidays plus a few other occasions during the year. (See Table 30.) Again there are a few unexpected differences. More fathers than sons attend regularly; twenty-five per cent of the former attend once a month or more, whereas 13 per cent of the latter do so. No one attends daily (unless in mourning). Fewer of the fathers than the sons fail to attend at all.

TABLE 30. Synagogue Attendance of Second and Third Generations

FREQUENCY	FATHERS		SONS	
	Number	*Per Cent*	*Number*	*Per Cent*
Once a week	12	14.3	4	4.8
Once a month	9	10.7	7	8.3
High Holidays and occasionally	24	28.6	21	25.0
High Holidays only	34	40.5	35	41.7
Never	5	5.9	17	20.2
Total	84	100.0	84	100.0

Significant: 4 d.f. chi-square = 11.01 P < .05 T = .18

There are no significant differences in ritual observance between fathers and sons. (See Table 31.) Most members of both generations practice minimum observance * (38 per cent of the fathers and 42 per cent of the sons). Maximum observance † is characteristic of 34 per cent of the fathers and 26 per cent of the sons. A few more sons than fathers observe no religious ritual. There is little concern in either generation about rigorous adherence to traditional religious practice. Most of the younger nonobservers are indifferent

TABLE 31. Ritual Observance of Second
and Third Generations

OBSERVANCE	FATHERS		SONS	
	Number	*Per Cent*	*Number*	*Per Cent*
Maximum observance	29	34.5	22	26.2
Minimum observance	32	38.1	35	41.7
No observance	23	27.4	27	32.1
Total	84	100.0	84	100.0

Not significant: 2 d.f.   chi-square = 1.41   P > .05

to ritual, feeling no need to introduce religious tradition into the home at least until they have children to "appreciate" it. They anticipate practicing more religious observance in the future. Only a few reject all religious observance and they are closer to second generation than third in age and background. Their negative reaction to ritual is not typical of the third generation.

Orthodoxy was pounded into me with no good reasons given. I rebelled against that sort of education where

* Minimum observance includes lighting Friday night Sabbath candles and/or some acknowledgment of such holidays as Passover, Chanukah, and the High Holidays.

† Maximum observance includes reciting Kiddush (a benediction chanted over the cup of wine on Sabbaths and festivals) and/or observing dietary regulations in addition to the above-mentioned rituals.

there's no explanation given for anything. Just being a Jew is not reason enough to do all they say you should do. Now I deviate.

Rituals like kosher laws don't mean anything to me. Services are poor, not really spiritual. Just going to synagogue twice a year doesn't make you Jewish.

Most of the third generation look with approval on their religious tradition. Even those who are not yet observant plan to be when they have children. One respondent justified his religious behavior with,

I enjoy rituals. It compensates for some of life's more monotonous aspects to have them and something to believe in.

By and large, fathers and sons observe the same types of rituals. The more demanding practices such as observance of dietary regulations are more frequently followed by the fathers, but the differences are not significant. The most popular practices of both generations center around periodic holidays rather than regular observance—particularly those holidays oriented toward children in modern Judaism (e.g., Chanukah).

Of the sons who observe at least selected aspects of their tradition, 24 per cent claim they have always observed particular rituals. The religious observance of the rest begins with the acquisition of wives who "want to keep a Jewish home" or the arrival of children for whom religion is considered essential. The most frequently cited reason for the observance of certain rituals is, again, the fact that their families also observe them. (Forty-eight per cent give this reason.) The remaining reasons all focus on the children—i.e., rituals are somehow "good" for children, rituals have "survival value" and teach children what it means to be Jewish, or ritual practices are taught in Sunday School and the children insist that their parents observe them. Typical of this reasoning:

> Rituals are good for children. If you want them to be Jewish, you need customs to perserve it.

> I observe the holidays to please my sons who learn about them at Sunday School. My wife knows the appropriate prayers and it appeases my conscience.

> Ritual observance is important. It keeps Jewish tradition alive. What I will observe when I'm married depends on my wife.

> I feel the rituals have value in carrying on the culture. It's good for the family to know Jewish tradition.

The striking characteristic of the religious observance of both second and third generations is its convenience. It does not require the rigor of daily devotion nor set them apart from non-Jews. The accepted rituals are the ones which most closely approximate the religious practices found in gentile homes. Members of the younger generation are not unaware of the less-than-sacred aspects of their religious practices and acknowledge the expediency of their selectivity; they are content that no more is demanded of them.

> I observe these practices out of habit. All the people I know observe them. They're the convenient ones— they don't interfere with anything else.

> I follow the same practices my parents observed in their time for the children to remind them they're Jewish. These are the convenient ones, easy to begin to observe when the children are old enough to be aware of these things.

Of the sons, 90 per cent consider religious education important for children. Only 13 per cent of the respondents themselves had no religious education, and even fewer (10 per cent) do not intend for their children to receive religious instruction. But although they want their children to have some religious training, fewer choose to send them to the daily Talmud Torah than attended themselves. (Sixty-three per cent of the third generation went to Talmud Torah, whereas only 30 per cent send, or intend to send, their own children there.) An increasing number prefer Sunday School so that their children may obtain religion in easy Sunday doses.

Religious education thus continues to be regarded as important, but a less rigorous and traditional type is demanded, a type that is neither time-consuming nor likely to isolate Jewish children from non-Jews. As one respondent put it,

I don't want my children to get too much religious training—just enough to know what religion they're not observing. After all, gentiles know about it, so should Jews.

The function of such training for a majority of respondents (57 per cent) is to teach their children about their religion so that they know what Judaism is. The parents can no longer do it themselves; the transmission of the religious heritage now requires specialists.

The Talmud Torah is an improvement over the old orthodox ones. Children should learn about Jewish culture and history when they're young or they never will and they'll regret it later.

If they want to, children should be exposed to religious history and language. It's a good part of anyone's education, although ritual is not important today.

Children should have the opportunity for religious education. They're Jews and should know about it.

Another 16 per cent think that religious education helps to establish a child's identity so that he "knows what it means to be Jewish." The synogogue is asked to do what the family does not know how to do, i.e., make children in some way "feel Jewish" and accept their Jewishness.

I am interested in historical and cultural background for children, not in rituals and formal observance. A child should develop a feeling of comfort and pride in being Jewish, which I didn't have.

Religious training is important to a feeling of belonging so you're not lost at sea. It builds up confidence.

Everyone should have enough formal education to have information about his religion so he feels comfortable about his group. But children should be sent to Sunday School for information, not religious sentiment.

Another function attributed to religious education is ethical training.

Ethical training is important for children. And it's usually done through religious training. No other way has been established yet.

Other parents feel that their children should learn about religion now so they can make "intelligent" choices later in life about religious affiliation and handle situations that are likely to arise. Their reasoning is self-conscious and not a little defensive:

It's their right to know some religion so when they're adults they can choose to follow or ignore it. You have no real choice when you know nothing.

Parents should provide some direction, children can leave the religion later. If you let them make up their own minds, they usually do it on the wrong bases (like social pressures) because of lack of information.

Children should have some background information about religion and know they're Jewish so they can adjust to situations they're bound to encounter in the future, like anti-Semitism.

The remaining few parents offer a variety of social and pragmatic reasons for wanting their children to attend Sunday School.

Going to Sunday School is useful in the community we live in. It would be difficult for the children to understand why they don't go when others do.

Religious education is important socially. Children meet people in the same religion and form close friendships.

The acceptance of the value of religious instruction is so pervasive that even intermarried couples send their children to some sort of "liberal" Sunday School to learn about religion.

I belong to the Unitarian Society for the benefit of the kids. It's in accord with my convictions and it wouldn't be fair to my wife to make the kids Jewish in religion. They should have liberal religious education so they can decide later. They should get religious background in all religions.

Of the 10 per cent who do not approve of religious education for their children, only a handful are militant in their rejection. One atypical rebel, reminiscent of the more secular '30's, declared,

More damage is done to rational thinking by religious education than is accomplished.

Most of them, however, do not object to religious training in principle; they simply disapprove of teaching techniques or substantive emphases in present vogue. They are few in number, but vocal in dissent.

Religious education would be all right if they really taught religion and fostered an intellectual stimulation of interest in their culture. But they don't . . .

Really religious training is not available in Sunday School. Children aren't taught religious principles, just rituals and a little history.

They have archaic methods of teaching at the Talmud Torah, but my wife wants the children to go there. They shouldn't be submitted to it, but they should have some rational explanation of their religion.

Those who consider religious education important also think that children should be made "aware of being Jewish." The large majority feel that children should know who and what they are. The reasons offered in justification, however, are of two interestingly different types: positive and negative. The positive arguments claim that religious identity provides stability, enabling children to be proud of their heritage.

All children should be taught their identity, whether Jew or gentile.

A person must be attached to some religion for stability. It's good for people to adhere to it.

You should formulate some religious opinions for children so they'll have some religious preferences.

Children should know who they are and where they belong. Identity and roots give them stability.

It's stupid not to know where you come from even if you eventually go a different way. Being Jewish is part of what you are, you can't avoid awareness of it.

The negative side of the picture most frequently evoked is the need to establish one's own identity as a defense against external pressures, particularly those directed against minority-group members.

Others will make children painfully aware of being Jewish. They should be made aware at home in self-defense.

Living in a Protestant country, they will have it driven home to them anyway. They should learn not to be ashamed of being Jewish.

I want them to be aware from home of the good side of being Jewish. Others will make them aware of the bad side.

He's going to want to know where he fits in and other people will tell him. It's too bad, but he should know. We don't know how to accomplish it educationally yet.

Children should be brought up in some faith since other people make the association for the child. They identify him as Jewish because of his name. He should know what it is.

Children should have some affiliation so they don't feel they're different from others. He'll be different enough as a Jew. He'd be too different as an atheist.

They should be aware they're Jews so they'll have the answers to anti-Semitism and won't think they're any different from anyone else.

Only a few argue that awareness of Jewish identity is not necessary. They feel that children shouldn't be made self-conscious about being Jewish. After all, they're no different from anyone else. "Being Jewish is not something one must always be conscious of—I wasn't." By and large, however, Jewish identity is not regarded as a burden, or even as a determinant of life chances; thus there is little need to shed it.

The generally favorable attitudes toward religious education and Jewish identity are extended to specific rites of passage, the Bar Mitzvah (ceremony held for a 13-year-old boy when he becomes a "son of the commandment" responsible for upholding the law) or confirmation (graduation from Sunday School at the age of 15), as ceremonies which reinforce Jewish self-awareness. Eighty-six per cent of the third-generation sample have been Bar Mitzvah or confirmed, and 80 per cent plan to have their children Bar Mitzvah or confirmed.

While rituals are being preserved in modified form, much of the culture in which they were originally rooted grows less familiar to the third generation—if the decline in knowledge of Yiddish and Hebrew is any indication. Knowledge of Yiddish, the folk language of Eastern European Jews, declines strikingly from second to third generation. Only two respondents can speak Yiddish; another 25 understand some. Sixty-eight per cent, however, know no Yiddish at all, in contrast to the 16 per cent of the second generation who know no Yiddish. Even such knowledge of Hebrew as is necessary for following services is not universal among members of the third generation in spite of their Talmud Torah background. Forty-two per cent can read no Hebrew, and only 17 per cent read with understanding. The rest remember only enough to follow the liturgy.

The religious rebellion of the second generation lasted only until a third generation appeared on the scene. The older generation's adaptation of the synagogue to American life and its selective observance of tradition resolved the tensions created by a socially isolating orthodoxy and need for religious institutions to perpetuate Jewish identity. The third generation, raised in a watered-down, middle-class version of Judaism has little difficulty in accepting the religious resolutions of its fathers. Members of this generation join their fathers' Conservative and Reform synagogues and observe the same child-centered holidays.

The religious behavior of the third generation is the behavior of a generation that regards Judaism as "just a religion, a set of beliefs" which makes Jews "no different from other people." Young Jews continue to modify the practices of their elders so that they are further and further removed from traditional orthodoxy and in ever closer conformity to the religious behavior of the majority. Little of their religious behavior remains uniquely Jewish, except that they congregate with other Jews.

Although they are more traditional in attitude than practice, members of the third generation accept their obligation for at least nominal participation in religious institutions. They may attend synagogues less often than their fathers and observe fewer rituals, but they share the prevailing American climate of opinion favoring religious affiliation. Like their fathers before them, third-generation Jews want to pass on a religious identity to their children. Ironically, their emphasis on religious, rather than more broadly social, identification strengthens the synagogue at the expense of other Jewish institutions. Indeed, the more intellectual of them are choosing to be Jews on exclusively religious rather than historical, cultural, or communal grounds.

ACCEPTANCE

These then are the aspects of its fathers' world that the third generation accepts, albeit selectively. An institutional heritage as complex as this cannot be summarily accepted or rejected. Members of the third generation adopt their fathers' religious resolutions when they are consistent with the way of life they envision for themselves. They accept the older generation's economic resolutions when they support styles of life beyond the social reach of their elders. In sum, religion is acceptable as long as it is a highly acculturated one. Jewish occupations can also be tolerated as long as they are profitable and readily convertible into prestigeful job titles symbolizing a new way of life.

As young Jews organize their lives around new occupations and styles of life, rather than tribal affinities, Judaism becomes a specialized voluntary association in the manner of Protestant denominations. Accordingly, membership in the Jewish community may come to depend on more general social qualifications instead of ethnic birth and ritual purity. The gilded ghetto, however, remains an ethnic community with characteristics not calculated to appeal to a status-conscious third generation. Subject to the judgment of its heirs, the gilded ghetto may be tarnished by rejection.

7
The Philistines Rebel

THE CLASSIC TRADITION, posing a social dialectic between generations, judges a generation untrue to itself that does not rebel against the world of its elders. Thus far we have indicated only the extent of the third generation's acceptance of its fathers' patterns of behavior, a selective acceptance of behavior that does not violate its image of the good life. An analysis of the conflict resolutions that have been rejected suggests that the rebellion of the third generation, such as it is, occurs in the sphere of interpersonal relations. Since this is the area in which status factors operate most extensively, it is here that the greatest change in behavior is expected.

These "social" resolutions are integrally related to the "economic" resolutions already discussed, but we distinguish between them, perhaps arbitrarily, for purposes of analysis. It is quite clear, however, that the economic resolutions of the third generation are directly influenced by status factors. (For instance, the entry into traditionally non-Jewish occupations which are accorded more prestige in the general community than the occupations of the second generation.) Status factors influence both the choices the third generation makes and the ideology it formulates to justify them. The economic resolutions in turn influence the nature of the social resolutions. They provide the occupational reference groups whose styles of life are emulated by the third generation as well as the incomes that pay for them. The styles of life adopted by the third generation are increasingly influenced by its occupations.

Eighty-eight per cent of the third-generation sample are married and 93 per cent of these have Jewish wives (all but two of whom were born in the United States).[1] Close to half of the wives' parents were also born in the United States. Seventy-seven per cent of the respondents have children, with an average of 1.98 children per family. Most of the children are still of preschool age. Those who go to school have non-Jewish friends and belong to youth groups that include both Jews and gentiles. Since most of the respondents have small children, few of the wives work now (16 per cent), although 56 per cent have worked at some time in the past, mostly at secretarial and clerical jobs.

Where and how do these young married couples and their children live? Who are their friends? To what types of organizations do they belong? Table 32 summarizes the

TABLE 32. Social Resolutions of Second
and Third Generations

VARIABLE	SECOND GENERATION Per Cent	THIRD GENERATION Per Cent	SIGNIFICANCE OF ASSOCIATION WITH GENERATION
Live on North Side	34.5	5.9	Significant
Live in predominantly Jewish area	47.6	17.9	Significant
Have both Jewish and gentile friends	17.9	70.2	Significant
Memberships in Jewish clubs and organizations	69.0	63.1	Not significant

1. The five non-Jewish wives include three Protestants and two Catholics. The social characteristics of their husbands are not appreciably different from those who have married Jewish women.

observations on their social resolutions, revealing striking differences between fathers and sons.

A majority of the sons (48 per cent) were brought up in predominantly Jewish neighborhoods, but only 18 per cent live in Jewish neighborhoods now that they are married. (See Table 33.) Thirty-seven per cent of the fathers

TABLE 33. Religious Composition of Neighborhoods in which the Third Generation Grew Up, Lives Now, and Prefers to Live

NEIGHBORHOOD	GREW UP IN		NOW LIVE IN		PREFER TO LIVE IN	
	Number	Per Cent	Number	Per Cent	Number	Per Cent
Predominantly Jewish area	40	47.6	15	17.9	20	36.4
Predominantly gentile area	31	36.9	26	30.9	1	1.8
Mixed area	13	15.5	43	51.2	34	61.8
Total	84	100.0	84	100.0	55	100.0

No Preference 29 (34.5% of 84 sample)

Significant: 4 d.f.   chi-square = 49.87   P < .001   T = .334

live in gentile neighborhoods; they are the wealthier members of the second generation, who had few other alternatives at the time they left the area of first settlement. Fifty-one per cent of the sons live in what they consider "mixed" neighborhoods, usually suburbs in which the relatively low proportion of Jewish residents are sufficiently clustered on certain blocks to give the impression of greater numbers than there actually are.

Thirty-five per cent of the sons have no preference about the religious composition of their neighborhoods. It is not a factor they consider important in choice of residence. Rather, they look for "good" houses in "nice" neighborhoods. The physical characteristics of the neighborhood are more important than the religious; they can always seek friends outside the neighborhood. They reason this way:

> I'm now more concerned with the physical characteristics of a neighborhood. I used to want more Jewish neighbors since I missed having Jewish friends when I was young. But everyone now is more mobile; it's easier to get around and see friends outside the neighborhood.

"Niceness" is a status criterion that the old Jewish neighborhoods can't meet, and the younger generation is determined to find housing which appropriately reflects its status. Consequently, most members of the third generation look first for neighborhoods that are suitable both physically and socially, and worry later about whether or not there are any other Jewish residents.

Most of those who have a preference prefer to live in religiously mixed neighborhoods because it is "good for the children to learn to live with others." Mixed neighborhoods seem to them to approximate reality most closely.

> I prefer mixed areas and want to get out of all-Jewish neighborhoods. It helps to better understanding between Jews and gentiles since understanding develops in neighborly relations.

> I don't want a mostly Jewish neighborhood because it becomes ghettoized and then you live only with Jews.

> Children should learn early how to live in a mixed world.

> I prefer not to be in a single racial area. It's ridiculous to be with Jews only; you meet them anyway.

Children get a better outlook on life from mixed neighborhoods. They have to learn to deal with non-Jews in life.

Although many of the sons were brought up in gentile neighborhoods, only one of them prefers to live in one now. They believe their own children will be happier if they have Jewish friends in the neighborhood, something they missed in their own childhood. A surprising number, therefore, want to live in Jewish neighborhoods, but newer ones than the area of first settlement. These areas have the advantage of conveniently available Jewish facilities such as synagogues, Sunday Schools, and delicatessens (without the disadvantage of as many Jews as the North Side). They justify their preference with a recollection of earlier experiences in gentile neighborhoods.

You feel a certain isolation in a gentile neighborhood.

You're only a neighbor, not friends. It doesn't matter to me, but the children will need friends and these are likely to be Jewish.

I want to bring up my children in an area where they'll have Jewish friends. Also it's hard on the wife in a gentile area, where they just say 'nice day' but aren't friendly or neighborly. They're clannish.

I was brought up in a Jewish neighborhood and I find there's a friendlier feeling. I feel more comfortable there.

I want to live in a Jewish neighborhood to raise a family. . . . I want the kids to have some affiliation with a Jewish community, some Jewish tradition such as drive for college and certain occupations. These are the good parts of the heritage and are found more easily when you live with Jews.

The common characteristic of these justifications is their familistic orientation. Family life remains more rooted in tradition than other aspects of third-generation behavior and 36 per cent want their families flanked and shielded by Jewish neighbors.[2]

An overwhelming majority of the sons (94 per cent) have moved away from the predominantly Jewish North Side where many of them were brought up. Indeed, some of the fathers have also moved from the North Side since their children have grown up. Those who moved headed south and west for the suburbs. The third generation is most likely to live south, but the second generation may live either north or south.

At present, 74 per cent of the married third generation own their own homes, the average value of which is $21,181. The intentions for future residence of 70 per cent of the sons are either to remain in or move to the suburbs, particularly West Parricus, which they consider a good residential area. Here they expect to find enough Jewish friends and neighbors to benefit the children, but not so many that they are insulated from gentiles. West Parricus is the suburb with the highest proportion of Jews, but they are not predominant by any means. There are enough Jews to create a demand (now fulfilled) for a new synagogue, Sunday School, and youth center. And since some blocks are more "mixed" than others, people seeking homes there can have their choice of predominantly Jewish areas or mixed ones.

The suburban milieu is a new one for the traditionally

2. Interestingly, the preference for "Jewish" or "mixed" neighborhoods frequently refers to the same suburban area. Its definition as "Jewish" or "mixed" is a matter of social perception and the specific residential blocks under consideration. Thirteen per cent of the residents of West Parricus, for instance, are Jewish. For some respondents, this is enough to turn West Parricus into a "Jewish" neighborhood.

urban Jew. It is a setting so intent on the virtues of sociability that it brooks no strangers. No one can be in it, and
not of it; participation is the price of suburban residence
for Jew and gentile alike. The principle of *Gemeinschaft*
extends to all inhabitants. No longer protected from his
surroundings by the social isolation of the gilded ghetto,
the young Jew must respond to the demands of his community, conforming to the expectations of his neighbors
as neighbors rather than as Jews. He is drawn into a social
situation in which ethnic uniqueness is not recognized as
legitimate grounds for differential association. These are
communities organized around principles of status rather
than ethnic birth per se, although minority-group membership continues to operate as a determinant of status.

Along with the increasing shift to mixed neighborhoods,
there is a growing number of sons who have both Jewish
and gentile friends, in contrast to the disproportionate number of fathers who have only Jewish friends. Although 80
per cent of the sons include only Jews among their four
closest friends, 70 per cent have some gentile friends in
the larger social circles with whom they exchange social
visits. Among the fathers, 82 per cent have only Jewish
friends and are not on visiting terms with any gentiles.
(See Table 34.) Members of the third generation are likely
to have both Jewish and gentile friends, whereas members

TABLE 34. Religious Composition of the Friendships
of Second and Third Generations

FRIENDS	FATHERS		SONS	
	Number	*Per Cent*	*Number*	*Per Cent*
Mostly Jewish friends	69	82.1	25	29.8
Both Jewish and gentile friends	15	17.9	59	70.2
	84	100.0	84	100.0

Significant: 1 d.f.　　chi-square = 46.76　　P < .001　　phi = .594
　　　(c = 0)

of the second generation are likely to have no gentile friends.

Fifty-six per cent of the sons claim to have no preference about whether or not their friends are Jewish. Another 34 per cent prefer to have Jewish friends, and 10 per cent voice an explicit preference for both Jewish and gentile friends. Those who prefer Jewish friends are quick to explain themselves, for the expression of a "discriminating" preference is not condoned in the self-consciously tolerant suburbs (although most people interact on the basis of some selectivity). A variety of reasons are offered in justification—for instance, the comfortable intimacy they find with other Jews. And besides—as they defensively point out—they don't get to meet non-Jews now that they're out of school.

> After you're married you tend to stick to your own kind since Jews have their own kind of life and share a common outlook.

> After school, I drifted away from my old friends. I made friends with my wife's friends who are all Jewish.

> I'm not making new friends now. I was brought up with Jews and I don't get to meet any gentiles now.

> I have only Jewish friends. I have no desire to avoid gentiles, but I don't meet them since I belong mostly to Jewish organizations.

> My social life is with Jews. I meet only Jews. There's a social wall separating Jew from gentile and their social lives are different.

> I feel more intimacy with Jewish friends since there are more common bonds.

I prefer to have mostly Jewish friendships, though not exclusively. Experience has shown them to be longer lasting friendships.

I get along with Jews best. I'm not as comfortable with non-Jews. I don't have to strive for acceptance with them since I don't care what they think of me.

I prefer Jewish friends because I like them better. Those I like have a certain sensitivity and quality—a cynicism combined with compassion, a humor and irreverence. Only some gentiles, who are really misplaced Jews, share this quality. And they also prefer to associate with Jews.

Most respondents assume that the "democratic" ideology should preclude the operation of religion as a selective factor in the choice of friends (at least as an explicitly expressed factor). They are, therefore, less likely to defend their preference for religiously mixed friendship groups. Indeed, respondents born and bred in other cities complain of the in-grown and nonintellectual nature of the social life of North City Jews in contrast to the participation of Jews in mixed intellectual, professional, and artistic circles they have known elsewhere.

Judaism should be an intellectual principle, not a social principle. Jews shouldn't enclose themselves exclusively with other Jews.

It's more interesting and intellectually stimulating to be with people on the basis of shared interests.

Gentiles here are more intellectual. I feel a little more at ease with Jews, although the gentile friends I've chosen are those easy to get along with. I like being in different circles. Gentiles in North City are more interesting—the Jews are stodgy, rich, and live off their fathers. They see only each other.

> There's a forced camaraderie and association here
> among Jews. They're forced to cluster, but have noth-
> ing in common except business so they have nothing
> to talk about. I feel no need to associate with them.

These respondents are looking for a social life based on
shared interests rather than shared birth, an "interesting"
one rather than a traditionally enclosed one.

Being Jewish is no longer necessary or sufficient grounds
for association. The conviction of an older generation that
being Jewish was adequate qualification for friendship led
to as much stereotyping of Jews within the minority group
as in the majority group. Resisting the imposition of stereotypes by both in-group and out-group, young Jews cultivate social identities free of ethnic taint and turn to non-
Jews for personal recognition.

Paradoxically, while most young Jews claim to exercise
no religious preference in their friendship choices, an overwhelming proportion of friendships considered "close"
by the respondents involve other Jews. That they should
feel bonds of intimacy with these friends is understandable
in light of the fact that 62 per cent of the close friends are
people with whom they grew up. Since almost half of our
respondents grew up in Jewish neighborhoods, it is not
surprising that they feel they have most in common with
the Jews they knew in childhood. None of the close
friendships that have survived maturity include gentiles.
Wives' friends and general social activities are other
sources of Jewish friendships. Since most of the wives are
Jewish, the friends they introduce to the couples' social
circles are also likely to be Jewish.

The continued intimacy with childhood friends suggests
some reluctance to forfeit old social ties in the interest of
mobility. Unwilling to risk alienation from their origins,
young Jews who have not been uprooted by their jobs are

bound by the silver cord of old friendships to the Jewish community. The psychic cost of mobility is high for those who must break with the past, too high for some to incur willingly. The social segregation of the third generation, however, is neither as extensive nor as frustrating as that of the second generation. The in-group friendships of the former are not the necessary consequence of exclusion by non-Jews, but the result of shared interests with Jews (interests in which Judaism plays a negligible role). Although respondents feel they have most in common with their Jewish friends, it is not because of their shared ethnic birth.

Those respondents who include gentiles among their four close friends cite occupation and college as the two social settings in which such friendships are formed. They are the major sources of an increasing number of "mixed" friendships, but since these friendships are more recent and less "social" in origin, they are less likely to be considered intimate (although they meet the criterion of exchanging social visits). These are the contexts, however, in which values that by-pass traditional ethnic barriers are most likely to develop.

The apparently greater willingness of sons than fathers to cultivate friendships with non-Jews is obviously in large part because of increased opportunities to do so. More of the sons have non-Jewish colleagues. Equally important, the sons are more secure about engaging in social relations with gentiles; they have less cause to distrust them. Forty-six per cent have experienced no anti-Semitism in their own lives, or have encountered it only in the name-calling and gang fights of their North Side childhood. Another 27 per cent ran into some anti-Semitism in the armed service and in the casual remarks of others, but only 26 per cent have encountered discrimination in the more serious forms of social exclusion or occupational restriction. The majority of respondents, therefore, are little disturbed by anti-Semitism; it is not an immediate problem for them. As one respondent explains,

> I'm not bothered by anti-Semitic remarks. They're made by ignorant people. I'm much more bothered by the Jews' anti-gentile behavior. They're more discriminating than gentiles.

In accord with their lack of personal experience with anti-Semitism, 60 per cent of the sons feel that the Jews in North City are well accepted by the general community. They can afford, therefore, to attempt more extensive social interaction with non-Jews—providing, of course, they have the opportunity to do so. Many complain that they would like to know more gentiles, but rarely meet them.

Along with growing interest in social relations with the majority group, there remain certain in-group tendencies. Nowhere are the in-group pressures stronger than in the area of marriage choices. Although two-thirds of the sample once dated gentile girls, 87 per cent preferred to marry a Jewish wife, either because of family pressures (52 per cent) or because they felt there would be fewer marital problems (48 per cent). (Of those married, 93 per cent actually have Jewish wives.) Few offer any clearly formulated reasons for their decided preference for religious endogamy. This is simply the way things have always been, as far as they are concerned. Marriage is, after all, the ultimate and most intimate form of social acceptance, and even young Jews are uncertain about their status with gentiles and ambivalent about acknowledging them as peers.

> I was brought up that way in my environment. It's just not kosher to marry a gentile and I never thought differently.

I have irrational feelings about intermarriage. It's just not done. I almost married a superior type of non-Jewish nurse myself, but I decided against it and I'm not sure why. Maybe because it's too good for the *goyim* (having a Jewish husband, that is).

Their ambivalence is projected into the future; sixty-nine per cent disapprove of intermarriage for their children as well. Some are indifferent or don't know how they would react to such a hypothetical situation. Only 10 per cent would actually give the intermarriage their parental blessings, or at least accept it, although none of the others anticipate sitting in mourning for the intermarried offspring as the orthodox first generation did. Most of those who object to the prospect of intermarriage suspect they would accept it after it was a *fait accompli*.

In sum, we find that the more intimate the social relationship, the more likely it is to be an in-group, or Jewish, relationship. Mixed relationships remain peripheral to the third generation's social life, although they are growing in number and desirability.

Although more sons than fathers engage in informal social relations with non-Jews, there is no statistically significant difference between the generations in the proportion of memberships in Jewish as opposed to the non-Jewish or mixed clubs and organizations. (See Table 35.) The differences that do occur, however, are in the predicted direction. Sixty-nine per cent of the fathers' memberships are in Jewish organizations in contrast to 63 per cent of the sons' memberships. More of the sons' memberships than the fathers' are in mixed organizations, 37 per cent as compared to 31 per cent. Fewer sons than fathers belong to no organizations at all.[3] The sons belong to an

3. A significantly higher proportion of wives' organizational memberships, 76 per cent, are Jewish ones, suggesting their more limited contact with the general community. Fewer of their or-

TABLE 35. Religious Affiliation of the Organizational
Memberships of Second and Third Generations

TYPE OF CLUB	FATHERS		SONS	
	Number	Per Cent	Number	Per Cent
Jewish clubs and organizations	116	69.0	113	63.1
Non-Jewish or mixed clubs and organizations	52	31.0	66	36.9
Total *	168	100.0	179	100.0

1 d.f.   chi-square = 1.34   P > .05

* The data were multiple punched so that the totals represent number of memberships rather than number of respondents in the sample. Seventeen of the fathers and five of the sons belonged to *no* organizations.

average of 2.26 clubs and organizations, probably fewer than their fathers since they are just beginning to join as their incomes increase and their interests expand.

There are important qualitative differences in the organizational affiliation of the two generations. There are more memberships among fathers than sons in town and country clubs (which are exclusively Jewish) and in fraternal organizations such as the Masons (usually in a predominantly Jewish lodge). The sons, younger and less established, cannot afford the cost of such memberships as yet. Many, however, look forward to joining them in the future. At present they belong to B'nai B'rith lodges, the young married clubs of synagogues, and often to service organizations (particularly those aiding youngsters). They belong to these all-Jewish organizations more frequently than do their fathers. Such organizations, regardless of their explicitly stated purposes, function as social clubs for members of

ganizational memberships are non-Jewish, and more wives than husbands belong to no organizations at all.

the third generation, permitting them to get together with others of similar age and interests. In B'nai B'rith, for instance, they meet their friends for bowling once a week. (Most of them, as a matter of fact, give this as their sole reason for joining.) These organizations are, in other words, the functional equivalent of the town and country clubs of the older generation, whose membership fees are too expensive for the young married budget.

None of the respondents is actively affiliated with any Zionist organization, although most of them have a generally favorable attitude toward Israel. Thirty-seven per cent feel relatively indifferent toward Israel, arguing that they are not personally affected by its existence as a state. The others feel either some emotional involvement or a more detached interest in it. Although they are not committed to Zionism as part of the local status hierarchy of Jewish organizations, they do have the sympathetic interest in Israel characteristic of most Americans.

Although 55 per cent of the sons belong to only or mostly Jewish organizations primarily for "social" reasons, the types of memberships maintained by the growing minority who belong to non-Jewish or mixed organizations are of special interest to us. Already 39 per cent are in this category. In far greater number than their fathers, these sons have joined professional and business organizations. They are in occupations structured by interest groups and associations concerned with maintaining (or improving) the status and standards of their respective fields. They also belong more frequently to political organizations. The nonsectarian affiliation of the third generation is thus primarily in the occupational and political spheres rather than the social, a pattern analogous to the one found in its friendships. These memberships, however, can and do lead to shared interests and informal association with gentiles, which is one of the reasons these organizations appeal to the third generation. The obvious reason for nonparticipation in mixed social clubs is that few such clubs exist; the non-Jewish social clubs continue to exclude Jews.

There is some ambivalence among the members of the third generation as to the allegiance they owe to the Jewish community and its institutions. Exactly half of the respondents feel they should belong to Jewish organizations; the other half feel free not to affiliate with the organizations of the minority community. Similarly, 38 per cent prefer to participate mostly in the Jewish community, 21 per cent in the general community, and 30 per cent concede to the dual set of pressures by participating in both the Jewish and general communities.

One form that Jewish identification takes is a commitment to the minority community that obviates the significance of any but ethnic ties. Those who feel impelled to participate in the Jewish community express some vague feelings of obligation to it (which sometimes veil vested interests in it). These obligations do not require more explicit definition since they are in accord with the strong pressures for affiliation exerted by the community.

> A lawyer has obligations to his community. B'nai B'rith does community work. These Jewish philanthropies also provide contacts for me.

> I'm still Jewish in the eyes of others, therefore I remain Jewish and owe some obligation to the Jewish community, even if I've neglected it in the past.

> I prefer to participate in the Jewish community because I get more of a homey feeling with my own group of friends who are all Jewish.

> I feel some obligation to support Jewish service activities. I still have some Jewish identification.

Objections to exclusive participation in the minority community are less ambiguous. These are the rebels against the institutionalized pressures for in-group behavior who deny any common interests with members of organizations whose only reason for existence is their "Jewishness." Their interests lie elsewhere.

> I join organizations on the basis of common interests, not to play cards or bowl. I have no common interests with these people.

> I pick activities on the basis of my interests rather than on the basis of the religious affiliation of the organization.

> I have no particular interest in Jewish organizations which operate only in terms of fund-raising.

> I don't feel strongly affiliated with Jewish affairs and social activities. Cultural interests are important to me and these are not the basis of these Jewish organizations.

> I don't feel clannish or insecure and afraid to get out of the ghetto. I'm proud of our heritage, but I don't believe in ghettos and organizations only for Jews.

> I don't feel it's a duty to belong to Jewish organizations. I don't like the way they're run—they're too kikish. I don't mind giving money, but I don't want to work with them. It's a racket anyway. More money goes into expense accounts than to help their cause.

Preferences for formal affiliation with the general community are elaborately rationalized. There is no place for a "separate, but equal" Jewish community in the social lives of these "modern" respondents. Participation in the affairs of the general community is one way, in their minority opinion, to improve Jewish-gentile relations. Above all, such participation minimizes the deprivation of status associated with ethnic birth.

> The idea of a Jewish community has no place today. An individual in our age group has little racial tendencies and hasn't run into anti-Semitism. He has no reason to withdraw into a Jewish community. Jews lack diplomacy. They mean well and try to get along with others, but they have no insight into other people.

> I don't think there's a place today for a 100 per. cent Jewish community. It causes anti-Semitism. Jews should make an effort to get into other groups and get to know others.

> It's important that Jews contribute and be active in the broader community (like youth work, YMCA) and actively further Jewish-gentile relations.

> Social relations are confined enough to Jews. I don't want to be confined to them entirely, so I join general community work.

> Jews are too tight a social group here. They don't try to integrate and they create problems for themselves. They're prejudiced themselves.

> I have no desire to participate in the Jewish community. Socially I'm in contact with my professional colleagues. I'm revolted by those who fit the Jewish stereotype.

There remains an echo of "self-hatred" in the sensitivity to the subtleties of status. Respondents who have become sophisticated in the ways of a gentile world object to the stereotypical second-generation Jew as vehemently as their fathers objected to the "greenhorn" of the first generation. They do not yet speak for all of the third generation, but they are a vocal minority wary of any social characteristics that distinguish Jew from gentile, particularly those that might impede the development of peer relations (i.e., the despised characteristics that make a Jew a "kike," frequently associated with his marginal retail trade). Above all, these respondents are disturbed by by discriminatory practices on the part of the Jews that contribute to their own social segregation. Exclusion is bad enough; self-exclusion is intolerable.

Several of the husbands note that their wives are more "social-minded" and anxious to "get ahead" than they are. But this wifely urge for mobility rarely includes a desire to loosen the family's ties to the Jewish community. Except for a small minority of women whose academic and professional background is much the same as their husbands', most of the distaff side remains firmly rooted in the Jewish community, perhaps because of the social tribute paid them there. Few ethnic groups accord such importance to their women. Traditionally cherished and protected, the wives have less contact with gentiles than their husbands. Their neighboring with gentiles is casual and they have few organizational and fewer, if any, occupational sources for meeting gentiles. Any college friendships with gentiles have not survived married life and a divergence of communal interests. The sources affording opportunities for the husbands to associate with gentiles are less available to wives, whose range of interests and social relations is confined to the in-group.

The large majority of the respondents (84 per cent) are Democratic in their political preference (based on their vote in the 1956 national election). This preference, however, is based on the "liberal" outlook of "intellectual" groups rather than on traditional minority-group support of the Democratic Party. The Democrats, after all, have twice supported an "egghead" as candidate for President.

The leisure-time activities of the third generation are little different from those of their non-Jewish suburban neighbors. No one seems to be pursuing scholarship at the cost of his social or athletic interests. Activities that can be classified as "social" (visiting, organizational work, playing cards, etc.) are mentioned most frequently as leisure-time pursuits (36 per cent) and "athletic" activities (golf, bowling, etc.) are next in frequency (28 per cent). Activities centering around the home (hobbies, gardening, etc.) are also popular pastimes, whereas "cultural" activities (concerts, museums, reading, etc.) are least frequently pursued at leisure. Members of this generation are young, sociable, suburban Jews, innocent of giving grounds for any stereotype of Jewish "bookishness." They seek social acceptance, no less influenced than anyone else by contemporary culture heroes with well-adjusted, "other-directed" personalities. Indoctrinated in the good neighbor policy, they are susceptible to the suburban climate of sociability.

In keeping with the relative absence of cultural interests, only 1 per cent belong to any form of study group (e.g., private reading and book reviewing groups, Public Library Great Books discussion groups, or synagogue-affiliated groups studying subjects of Jewish content). Another 6 per cent attend the university lecture series or special classes. Most respondents read only a few novels and magazines during the course of a year. Only 17 per cent belong to any book clubs and another 7 per cent read material of specifically Jewish content, such as Jewish periodicals or novels about "Jewish" life and problems. Others have time only for keeping up with their professional reading. Reading habits are hardly an adequate index of intellectuality, but they do suggest a pattern of interests (or lack of them).

Some 23 per cent subscribe either to the symphony, the

Artists' Series sponsored by the university, or to the university theater. Or they are members of one of the art museums in the city. A few more attend some of these events irregularly without subscription. The large majority, however, in no way support local cultural institutions. To account for this requires a separate study, but the history of these institutions provides a clue to why the Jews of North City are less active in the arts than might be expected. *Kultur* in North City has long been a monopoly of the old Yankee elite. The groups supporting and patronizing the arts are not so much special interest organizations, whose memberships include all those with the appropriate interests, as they are social clubs excluding all but the members of a particular elite. Consequently, few others have had an opportunity to develop an active commitment to cultural institutions.

The informal ties to the Jewish community remain strong. Familial relationships, traditionally closely knit, are among those that keep the younger generation within the fold. Ninety per cent of the respondents have immediate family in North City and 94 per cent visit or keep in touch with them regularly. Even more significant, over half of the respondents continue to consult their parents on such major decisions as large purchases, moving, jobs, and education of children. They take for granted a continuing closeness with the family, seeking aid from them when the need arises. Even those whose jobs have taken them far from their roots try to sustain some semblance of familial intimacy with regular exchanges of correspondence.

Eighty-five per cent have no preference about whether or not the professional men they patronize are Jewish. Most of them, however, do see Jewish professionals since they "have always been in the family" or are personal friends. A few seek Jewish professionals because they feel more comfortable with them or because they think they're better or should be helped because it's more difficult for them to get clients.

Since so many of the respondents come from business families with extensive contacts, there are few who have not bought things at a "discount," usually from friends and relatives in the business (e.g., furniture, electrical appliances) rather than from discount houses. In reply to a question on buying habits, most respondents laughed and asked, "What Jew can't get something wholesale?" They claim, however, that such "bargains" are no longer a distinctive monopoly of Jews. They can buy at a discount without fear that it reflects their ethnic background since discounting has become a national pattern in the distribution of goods. "Everyone's getting it wholesale today, so why shouldn't we?"

Although the respondents avoid behavior patterns they consider distinctively Jewish, 58 per cent object to anyone who attempts to "assimilate" or deny his Jewish identity. By and large, members of our sample appear to follow the American middle-class pattern of life without being much troubled by their religious identity. The ideology that prevails is that they are no different from non-Jews, except in religious affiliation. Some 66 per cent feel that being Jewish is simply a matter of being a member of a religious denomination, a denomination that is ascribed by birth rather than taken on by choice.

> Being Jewish is a circumstance of birth—something you live with. You're born into a religion and brought up with it. You do what you want with it.

> Being Jewish shouldn't mean too much. We're just like other people. I don't like this Jewish self-consciousness and militancy.

> I don't feel Jewish in any way. I was just born Jewish.
> It doesn't make much difference to me.

> I was born and raised a Jew. That's my religion and
> that's how everyone regards me.

So circumscribed is the influence of religion in the lives
of third-generation Jews that only some perceive any of
the social consequences of being Jewish. One respondent
recognized that Judaism is more than a religious affiliation
in this way:

> I am a member of a social group as well as a religion.
> Being Jewish has broader social connotations that it
> should have.

Seventeen per cent define Judaism more broadly as a cultural heritage, a way of thinking.

> Being Jewish is a general feeling, set of attitudes, a
> way of thinking. You think of yourself as a Jew and
> see the world as divided into Jewish and gentile. You
> identify with the Jews.

Few find their major decisions influenced by being Jewish, but some continue to "feel Jewish" because others
regard them as Jewish or because they have some identity
with Jews.

Sixty-six per cent of the respondents feel they are "less
Jewish" than other members of the North City Jewish
community because, in their own opinion, they are "not as
religious," i.e., they attend synagogue and/or observe
ritual less frequently than they think others do. As long as
Judaism is defined only as a religious affiliation, the self-
image of the Jew is formulated in terms of religious ob-

servance. Those whose religious practices are minimal no longer have other grounds for identification as Jews.

> I'm socially set apart from these people because I'm not religious and I don't belong to a synagogue. I have no need for this type of religious affiliation.

Another 8 per cent feel they know less about Judaism than others do. Twenty-nine per cent claim they are no "more or less Jewish" than other Jews—they see themselves as typical young Jews. Some, particularly those from other cities, believe they are less confined to exclusively Jewish associations than most North City Jews.

> I'm different from North City Jews in my entire social life as well as in my beliefs. I am not so exclusive that I associate only with Jews.

> I don't want to be like the kikes who are ghettoized and losing their ideals and values of Judaism. They're only interested in making money—and seeing each other to talk about it.

Since most members of the third generation regard their Jewishness strictly as a religious matter, we expect that few will feel that it has had much of an effect on their lives. Thirty per cent claim that being Jewish has made no difference whatsoever to them.

> Being Jewish has made no difference. If I had the same family and connections, I would have turned out the same since that's what makes a difference.

Another 21 per cent think it probably has made a difference, but they are not certain how. Forty-eight per cent believe, realistically enough, that they have been most affected in the social and occupational spheres, i.e., they have mostly

Jewish friends and are in typically "Jewish" occupations. Although some acknowledge certain occupational restrictions due to being Jewish, only one respondent reacts to all such limitations with the bitterness characteristic of the rebels of past generations.

> I react with resentment to being Jewish. I'd prefer being like the rest of the people. I take no pride in being Jewish. I feel only discomfort at not being part of the majority. I feel it's a great limitation.

A few others find that being Jewish encourages a certain intellectuality or a drive for achievement, but, by and large, the social ramifications of a Jewish identity have little saliency for a generation relatively untouched by deprivation.

> Jews have the advantage of studying harder to be good students.

> You become more ambitious and aggressive as a Jew. You have to be twice as good as anyone else to get anywhere.

Some of the more self-consciously introspective and articulate respondents are aware of the psychological consequences of being Jewish. Consciousness of being Jewish, of being a member of a minority group, influences the total outlook of these respondents; the effects are so pervasive as to defy immediate detection.

> It makes a difference to belong to any group. You're classified by some people for their purposes, but you're no more limited by being Jewish than by being anyone else. Everyone's excluded from something.

> It shapes every attitude. Jews have the classic guilt complex and insecurity from persecution. These at-

titudes affect your relations with gentiles and make you hypersensitive and critical.

I feel Jewish all the time so I must act Jewish in some way.

Being Jewish has to affect you. It probably helps formulate the personality, it affects the social group in which you live, the clients you get in the office.

Anyone's background influences them. . . . It's sometimes uncomfortable to be a member of a minority group and part of a category of people that is disliked. It makes you self-conscious about being Jewish.

I'm conscious of myself as a Jew in a gentile society. The gentile doesn't have to adapt to such a condition. The Jew is forced to a greater awareness of himself in his social life.

Half of the sample was asked whether they thought there were any differences between Jews and gentiles. Sixty-two per cent claim there are no differences, except in religious affiliation, a cherished ideological position of the third generation. Another 16 per cent feel that Jews are in some way "nicer" and more moral; their family lives are in some way better. This claim to social superiority is perhaps the last trace of the "chosen people" concept; it certainly incorporates some of the popular images held by philo-Semitic Jews and gentiles alike.

Jewish family life is nicer. There's more respect for the female, more concern for the children. They concentrate on home life. There's little drinking.

There are more ties to the family. Jews want a better standard of living for their children. They have strong love for their children and are always trying to insure that their children have better opportunities and more advantages than they had.

Jews have a different attitude toward wives. They revere her more than gentiles do. There's more filial love and respect for parents also.

Others note that the distinctive characteristic of the Jew is the psychic burden he bears. Members of the majority group don't have to make certain psychological adjustments, which for the Jew often involve a defensive feeling of superiority. These responses, however, are not typical of an otherwise complacent generation.

A Jew is conscious of being marked as being different. This makes him different and more defensive.

The Jew's personality gets warped.

The Jew feels superior as a defense mechanism. He has strong in-group feelings.

Being a Jew in a gentile society makes for a difference in outlook. You're part of a minority.

In sum, the third generation chafes at the "Jewishness" of the gilded ghettos of its fathers. The achievements of the second generation, its acculturated but ethnic communities, are a source of conflict for the next generation; the class resolutions of one generation thus form the status tensions of the other. Members of the younger generation want to avoid their fathers' social resolutions, but seem uncertain how to go about it. They reject a social existence on the periphery of two worlds by moving to non-Jewish suburbs, joining mixed organizations, and cultivating more extensive social relations with gentiles. Their rejection, however, is not yet total—or perhaps not yet completed; the intimate core of their social lives remains Jewish.

The social patterns of members of the third generation are still in a state of flux. Their intentions surpass their actions. Although exasperated by the Jewish social life of their parents, they are at a loss to know how to change it. The tensions in this area remain largely unresolved, although attempts at resolution are consistently in the direction of rejection of social enclosure and avoidance of social uniqueness. Although they retain their religious identity, our young Philistines proudly proclaim themselves no different from anyone else.

One of the obstacles to the achievement of satisfactory social resolutions is the third generation's propensity for associating on the basis of shared ethnic origin, encouraging continued and exclusive interaction with Jews. Not many have yet developed interests that transcend the Jewish community, interests that identify individuals independently of any local community. Nevertheless, behavior that is class-linked in the second generation (that is, the "non-Jewish" behavior of upper-status older Jews) is more widely dispersed in the third generation. The structure of the Jewish community has changed in such a way that Jews are increasingly stratified by the same criteria that differentiate the general community. Commitment to traditional Jewish values is no longer a meaningful basis for class and status distinctions among young Jews.

One of the difficulties of the third generation may be a matter of perception. The sons regard their fathers' way of life as more Jewish than it actually is. Members of the third generation, for instance, report a much greater use of Yiddish among their fathers than is actually found in our second-generation sample (who use it only to add flavor to anecdotes or withold information from the *Kinder*). Their image may well be distorted by selective childhood memories of fathers so different from others, they even spoke a foreign language. The discrepancy in reported use of Yiddish (among other things) is perhaps less a function of the disparity between perception and reality than the difference in social origins of the samples. The second-generation sample represents a selected high- and low-status group; the fathers of the third-generation sample, randomly drawn, represent the full range of social strata in the Jewish community.

Young Jews' most vivid memory of their fathers is an unkind one of men so busy earning all that money could buy for their children, they had little time to be "companionable." The more guilt the fathers experienced for "neglecting" their children, the harder they worked to buy them off—and the more implacable the children grew. Some of the sons have still not forgiven their fathers for devoting long hours to business rather than the "finer things in life," like their children. Although the men of the third generation accuse their fathers of ignoring issues of status and style of life, our study of members of the second generation finds they become highly aware of the social utility of money, once they can afford the luxury of sensitivity to status judgments.

Thinly disguised in all the "idealistic" objections of the third generation to paternal "materialism" is a fundamental opposition to the exclusively Jewish status audience of the second generation. Young Jews reject the social exclusiveness of their elders. They want out, but can't find the exit—and it's much easier to blame their fathers than themselves.

OCCUPATIONAL FRONTIERS

Table 36 summarizes, in qualitative terms, the similarities and contrasts in the tension resolutions of the second and third generations. This capsule presentation of the characteristic behavior patterns of both generations reveals the extent to which the findings substantiate our major hypotheses. Members of the third generation accept, or improve upon, the economic positions of their fathers. They also accept the religious institutions of their fathers, continuing, however, to modify them in the direction of greater conformity with the majority religion.

TABLE 36. Qualitative Summary: Economic, Religious, and Social Resolutions of the Second and Third Generations

SECOND GENERATION

THIRD GENERATION

ECONOMIC

1. Self-employed in trade, commerce, or manufacturing or employed in craft or service.

1. Independent or salaried professional or semi-professional or in father's business.

2. *Cheder* or grade school education.

2. College and post-graduate education.

3. Average annual income of $14,314.

3. Average annual income of $10,291.

RELIGIOUS

4. Belong to Conservative or Reform synagogues.

4. Belong to Conservative or Reform synagogues.

5. Attend synagogue on High Holidays and/or occasionally.

5. Attend synagogue on High Holidays and/or occasionally.

6. Observe periodic, child-oriented rituals.

6. Observe periodic, child-oriented rituals.

7. Speak Yiddish.

7. Do not speak Yiddish.

SOCIAL

8. Live on the North Side in predominantly Jewish neighborhoods.

8. Live in suburbs in mixed neighborhoods.

9. Have only Jewish friends.

9. Have both Jewish and gentile friends, but close friends Jewish.

10. Belong mostly to Jewish organizations.

10. Belong mostly to Jewish organizations, with increasing number of non-Jewish occupational associations.

In the social sphere, the third generation is attempting to effect some change in the prevailing patterns of the second generation, but with varying degrees of success. Perhaps the significance of these findings lies in the unwillingness of the third generation to accept its fathers' social resolutions, rather than in the outcome of its experimentation with new social patterns. The social sphere is distinguished by its capacity to shake the complacent and comfortable acceptance of the younger generation.

Not all members of the third generation are responding in the same way to the world of their fathers. Some are more inclined to preserve the way of life characteristic of the gilded ghetto than others. What are the variations in the shared social experiences of this generation that account for the differences in their conflict resolutions? So far differences *between* generations have been explored rather than differences *within* the third generation.

Differences in chronological generation do not socially differentiate the members of a "sociological" generation who share the critical conditions of a common life situation. Nor does age alone distinguish between the "units" of the third generation. Those members of the third generation over 35 closely resemble their not much younger brothers under 35, except that they earn higher incomes and are more likely to be patrons of the arts. They are, in a word, able to afford the style of life to which younger Jews aspire, a style of life once characteristic of only upper-status second-generation Jews.

The introduction of chronological generation and age as intervening variables in our analysis has failed to disclose any significant differences in the behavior of those who grew up in the world of the third generation (perhaps because the subsamples are too small). Their socially shared experiences influence their behavior more critically than age or chronology.

A significant determinant in the lives of young Jews,

as in the lives of most young Americans, is occupation. Social variation within the third generation is produced by occupational differentiation. Many have entered their fathers' occupations, especially when it did not make economic sense not to do so. Their decision, however, rests not so much on the financial standing of the family business as on the invidious evaluation given it by the wider community. Members of the third generation are most likely to enter the family business when it is not a typically "Jewish" business.

Those who have chosen the more prestigeful occupations of the second generation maintain social ties to the established Jewish community, on whose good will much of their business or professional practice depends. Although they live in the suburbs, they have not moved far from the gilded ghettos of their childhood and are able to retain their old friendships. Because of these ties, they remain subject to the social control exercised by the established Jewish community and susceptible to the pressures for active participation. The common response of this "unit" within the third generation to its life situation is at least nominal participation in the institutions of the second-generation community.

Those who have not been limited to the occupational alternatives of the second generation have responded to their life situation in a way that further reduces the social and cultural differences between Jews and non-Jews. The occupations characteristic of this "unit" of the third generation have nationally oriented interests leading to the emergence of social structures that cut across the boundaries of ethnic groups and local communities. Jewish organization men, committed to the demands of their careers, are relatively free from the vested interests of any specific Jewish community. The geographic mobility required by their jobs encourages detachment from the institutions of the community of origin and permits the most effective escape from social visibility as Jews.

The organization men of the third generation are subject to the social influence of their colleagues rather than that of the Jewish community, and consequently, they are not readily characterized by any uniquely Jewish behavior or associations. Because they are in occupations that form status communities in which colleagues interact socially, their colleagues constitute a significant reference group that sets the norms for their shared style of life, a style of life not founded on "Jewish" content. Their social circles are mixed or non-Jewish, based on occupational and/or avocational interests rather than ethnic affiliation. Their organizational memberships also follow their interests rather than their birth.

The nature of the occupation, therefore, is significant in explaining differential participation in Jewish institutions and in-group behavior among third-generation Jews. Traditional Jewish occupations (family businesses in light manufacturing, wholesale and retail distribution, and independent professions) are contrasted with non-Jewish occupations (non-self-employed corporation executives, salaried professionals, and semi-professionals) in terms of attachment to the local Jewish community and its institutions. Those in traditionally non-Jewish occupations are theoretically expected to be more detached from the local community. In contrast, the social lives of those in Jewish occupations remain more securely tied to the minority community.

The subsamples are not as large as one might like, but third-generation Jews in North City are not yet widely distributed in non-Jewish occupations. Whether this is due to discriminatory employment practices or to lack of aspiration remains undetermined. Nevertheless, even with small subsamples, the social consequences of employment

in different types of occupations are striking. Table 37
summarizes the differences between those in Jewish occupations and those in non-Jewish occupations.

TABLE 37. Occupational Groups within the Third Generation

VARIABLE	PER CENT IN JEWISH OCCUPATIONS N = 63	PER CENT IN NON-JEWISH OCCUPATIONS N = 21	SIGNIFICANCE
Belong to or will join synagogue	95.2	71.4	Significant
Observe religious rituals	76.2	42.9	Significant
Best friends Jewish	85.7	61.9	Significant
Have some gentile friends	65.1	80.9	Not significant
Live in mixed neighborhoods	79.4	90.5	Not significant
Belong to mostly Jewish organizations	65.0	36.8	Significant
Feel should belong to Jewish organizations	61.9	14.3	Significant

Third-generation Jews in the salaried professions and
semi-professions are in every way less affiliated with the
Jewish community than those in traditional occupations.
Fewer Jewish organization men belong to a synagogue or
observe religious ritual. More of them include gentiles
among their four closest friends. Fewer of these men in non-
Jewish occupations belong only to Jewish organizations, and
even fewer feel that Jews *should* belong to specifically Jewish organizations. The majority of both types of occupational groups live in mixed suburban neighborhoods and
have some gentile friends.

The implications of these differences are far-reaching.
The behavior patterns of those in the new professions have
more than academic interest. They represent a highly
educated group of young men in occupations esteemed by
the dominant society who are increasingly "lost" to the
Jewish community. Although their accomplishments are

a source of pride to the in-group, they are regarded as a social luxury by other Jews as long as they fail to put their intellectual energies and services at the disposal of the minority community. One respondent, firmly entrenched in the in-group, speaks at least for the vested interests of the Jewish community when he asks, "What good is all their education if they don't participate in the community and put some of it to use for the Jews?" If it's not good for the Jews, it's not good—period.

Nevertheless, these professional men continue to regard themselves as Jews at least in so far as Judaism is the religion they were "born into." Since they are relatively unaffiliated with the institutions of the Jewish community, the source of their identification as Jews is more specifically religious rather than social, cultural, or historical. Professional Jewish fund-raisers and leaders of Jewish organizations are inclined, however reluctantly, to write this group off as a "lost cause." They would like to involve these unaffiliated young men more actively in Jewish affairs, if only for the potential prestige value of their participation, but the latter contribute little money and less time. Moreover, they are relatively transient, and local community leaders are never certain that particular salaried professionals are going to be living in the community long enough to be worth "cultivating." Synagogues also find that members of non-Jewish occupations are unlikely prospects, unless they have children of Sunday School age. Even then, they can rarely be seduced into active participation.

Jews in traditionally non-Jewish occupations are the social avant-garde of the third generation. Since they are formulating new types of social resolutions, their patterns of behavior offer the greatest contrast to those of the second generation. There is not yet a sharp differentiation within the youthful third generation in terms of income. There are, however, these occupational distinctions, absent in the second generation, which lead to significant social variations in the third generation. A new type of "intellectual" Jew is emerging, the salaried expert whose basic commitments are not to the Talmud and traditional Jewish institutions, but to his occupation and the status community of his colleagues.

Geographic mobility is a concomitant of these new occupations. Career opportunities are pursued in all parts of the country; advancing "vertically" frequently involves moving "horizontally," which further encourages detachment from any local ethnic community. And wherever he goes, the organization man has a built-in social life within his occupational circles. He has no need of the social resources of any local community. Members of the third generation who have moved to North City from elsewhere tend to be professional men (both independent and salaried, and usually specialists). A cross-tabulation of birthplace and occupation reveals that third-generation Jews born in North City are more likely to be found in traditionally Jewish occupations than in non-Jewish ones. Those born elsewhere are as likely to be in non-Jewish occupations as Jewish ones. Since many communities other than North City contribute personnel to the non-Jewish occupations represented in the sample, differences in behavior between those in non-Jewish and those in Jewish occupations are heightened.

The means of resolving the tensions of an exclusively Jewish social life are unequally distributed in the third generation. The tensions generated in the sphere of interpersonal relations are too great to go unresolved indefinitely. Now that the second generation has achieved economic security, the third generation seeks the appropriate social status and acceptance. Thus far only those whose occupational orientation extends beyond the boundaries of local ethnic communities have been able to develop social lives that rest on something other than religious identity. As social conditions change, however, so will the characteristic resolutions of the affiliated third generation. The major institutions of the established Jewish community are still the institutions of a second generation whose social ties are based on shared birth. They are a source of tension for the third generation and will be transformed as members of the younger generation come into their majority in the minority community, just as the institutions of the ghetto were transformed by the second generation. From the ethnic community of the second generation will emerge the status communities of the third generation founded on shared interests in styles of life.

8

The Grass Is Always Greener

As COMMUNITIES CHANGE, their members are freed from the constraints of tradition. The social anchorage of their lives shifts with the introduction of new norms and values. Changes in community life invite the members to seek new sources of identity, which in turn encourage further transformation of community structure. Nowhere are the processes of transformation and readjustment more evident than in the changing minority community. Here, individuals struggle to resist the unfavorable image of minority-group membership, frequently by simulating a world that white Anglo-Saxon Protestants take for granted. The resulting conflict is dramatic for Jews, for whom the imitation of gentile life is hampered by lingering survivals of ghetto existence.

The low status of first- and second-generation Jews in American society has been perpetuated by both their location in characteristic ethnic occupations and their protective insulation from the general community. Members of the second generation climbed the ladder of success in search of the best of two possible worlds. Prototypes of marginality, they sought access to non-Jewish values from within Jewish institutions. The "Jewishness" of the second generation hinged on a way of life founded on self-employment in traditionally Jewish occupations, commitment to such Jewish institutions as the synagogue and philanthropy, and exclusive association with other Jews. Friendship with gentiles was impeded both by the majority group's policies of exclusion and by the minority group's preference for the social bonds of shared birth.

The social world of the second generation is divided into two opposing camps, Jew and gentile, sufficiently inimical to bar the possibility of a friendly meeting ground. Nothing can be "good" for the Jews if it is "good" for the gentiles. The marginal men of this generation apply different social principles to their relations with Jews and non-Jews. Principles of tribal affinity form the basis of their associations with other Jews, while an ancient enmity colors their relations with gentiles. Underlying the façade the gilded ghetto presents to the gentile world is a latent fear of the out-group, combined with a muted sense of superiority. Although eager to court the favor of gentiles, second-generation Jews are beset with a complexity of ambivalent attitudes scarcely calculated to win the acceptance of non-Jews.

The problems of the third generation have changed with the conditions of the times, and it attempts to resolve them with the new means available to young Jews. Lacking any compelling social or historical justification for a separate identity, the third generation confines the scope of its Jewishness to a religious affiliation. Judaism no longer has the power to define a way of life for them. In this respect they are akin to the old German Jews, who rejected not their religious identity, but the idea of a separate social identity. Like the Germans, third-generation Jews are eager to disqualify themselves from membership in the ethnically segregated community. They are beyond the pale of ordinary Jewish mortals.

Although the family resemblance to its sociological forefathers is strong, the younger generation encounters new social and economic conditions. A critical change in the life situation of third-generation Jews is the occupational demand for highly trained experts. Nepotistic Jewish businesses, always a source of financial security, if not of intellectual excitement, are losing their educated heirs to employment in a gentile world of nationally organized occupations. The locus of identity is shifting accordingly from the community of birthright to the status community of shared style of life. The audience to whom the third generation addresses its status strategies is a demanding one of professional peers and colleagues. No longer does it play exclusively to the indiscriminate applause of Jewish friends and relatives. Although still held in affection, loving kin do not have the competence to render the kind of expert judgment necessary to ambitious young organization men.

The style of life of the second generation rests largely on what it can afford to buy. But like other young people, the third generation adopts more general occupational determinants of life styles. Even those who have stepped into the economic shoes of their successful fathers spurn the typically Jewish style of life that goes with the business. The good life that members of the third generation aspire to is shaped less by income than interests. They operate in the social spheres defined by the institutional contexts of the general society rather than those of the Jewish community.

The young Philistines of the third generation are contemptuous of paternal preoccupation with money at the same time that they profit from the fruits of their fathers' labors. They affect a rationale of refined sensitivity in contrast to the vulgar, mink-clad tastes of their fathers.[1] Although they do not yet possess the kind of wealth characteristic of high-status second-generation Jews, members

1. Ideologies such as these provide an important clue to the values and aspirations of a generation whose way of life is not yet crystallized.

of the third generation have in some respects modeled themselves after their rich elders—perhaps in the hope that the sins of the fathers will be visited upon the sons. Both are "non-Jewish" at least in so far as they live in non-Jewish neighborhoods, belong to non-Jewish organizations, and have non-Jewish friends. Although young Jews have less. money than their fathers, they have unprecedented access to non-Jewish occupations. The gentile values the second generation had to buy at a dear price the third generation has acquired on the job as a matter of course. The extent of acceptance by gentiles remains moot for both generations. Second-generation Jews, no matter how rich, were never able to rise above their ethnic identity. Their third-generation sons can at least achieve occupational status outside the Jewish community.

Upper-status life in the second generation foreshadowed much that was to characterize the next generation. Behavior found only among the wealthy in the older generation has filtered down to other strata in the third generation. The role model bequeathed by rich fathers has been inherited even by sons outside the line of direct financial descent. The exclusively Jewish values typical of low-status members of the second generation are perpetuated, in modified form, only by those sons still in traditionally Jewish occupations, regardless of economic standing. Merchants and manufacturers, old and young alike, continue to be identified as "Jewish" Jews, still an epithet of opprobrium that can de-status even the richest "Fagin with a tape measure." "Non-Jewishness" is a state of nirvana enjoyed by those whose occupations permit evaluation independent of minority-group membership. Plumbers who are transformed into sanitary engineers, junkmen who turn into metal brokers, even rabbis who undergo metamorphosis into Ivy League clergymen, all become eligible for the ranking system of the general society.

New means of livelihood are a necessary, but not sufficient qualification for acceptance in the gentile world. An intellectual knowledge of alternatives paves the way for making the "right" choices in life styles. North City Jewry is distinguished by its failure to exhibit much intellectual activity at any class level. Here is a community founded on the learned tradition of Talmudic scholarship, whose members find little time to read books, attend concerts, or visit art museums. They are thus all the more limited in the resources with which they confront the dilemmas of minority-group membership.

There is little local artistic color in the North City Jewish community. Perhaps it is the climate of the Midwest that is not congenial to bohemian society. If there are any "arty" residents or "upper Bohemians" (i.e., arty people with money), they make themselves scarce to public view, most unlikely behavior for such strata in the general community. If such circles existed at all among North City Jews, they have been depopulated by mobility and marginality. They have either moved out or remained peripheral to the local community since their values cannot be "turned into the universally acceptable coin" [2] of organizational affiliation and participation.

Indeed, intellectuals constitute a threat to the established community structure. Although the traditional Jewish community once cherished the values of scholarship, it was a sacred scholarship that supported the ancient orthodoxies. But the secular orientation of many contemporary intellectuals is one that defies the social introversion of the ethnic community. Intellectuals (even pretenders to intellect) make available alternative values that can serve as impetus for social change. The enclosed community, de-

2. We are indebted to Theodore Caplow and Reece McGee for this felicitous phrasing. See *The Academic Marketplace* (New York, Basic Books, 1958), p. 164, for an analogous example of the disruptive influence of intellectuality.

siring stability at all costs, cannot afford to reward the initiator of change. The studied indifference of North City Jews to intellectual achievement, shabby treatment of wit though it may be, protects the community from the shock of reality. (The prestige of professional men among Jews is not to be confused with an appreciation of intellectuality.) Complex historical factors account for the frenzy of organizational activity in the Jewish community, but its stunted intellectual growth can best be explained by fear of disrupting the comfortable status quo.

The unhappy consequence of this lopsided development of the community is the limitation imposed upon life alternatives. A new occupation appears to the ambitious as the only path to the "good life." Communities can, of course, be sufficiently flexible to permit the option of a "deviant" modus vivendi, but the insecurity of the vested interests in the North City Jewish community overrides parental permissiveness. Those anxious to preserve the existing social structure pose a difficult dilemma for the younger generation in starkly drawn terms. The sons must somehow choose between undivided loyalty to the local community and dedicated commitment to a career.

IDENTITY: AMERICAN DREAM AND JEWISH DILEMMA

There are few Jewish communities so well organized for perpetuity as the one in North City; nowhere else does the young Jew run so great a risk of being impaled on the horns of the minority dilemma. In this respect, the 20,000 Jews of North City are not entirely typical of America's five and one-quarter million Jews, 55 per cent of whom are found in New York, Philadelphia, Chicago, and Boston.[3]

3. Alvin Chenkin, "Jewish Population in the United States, 1958," *American Jewish Year Book*, 60 (1959), 3-19. Actually, if the metropolitan areas were included, the figure would probably be as high as 75 per cent.

The Jewish community of North City is sufficiently large to permit the development of a complex institutional structure parallel to that of the larger community, but not large enough to allow many to escape the network of institutional affiliation. It is a middle-sized community in which membership is defined by organizational participation.

The social life of North City's Jewish community, like that of the general community, is built around clubs and organizations founded on principles of exclusiveness whose influence extends even to such areas of rationality as the economy. The active social participation that is the prerequisite of membership in this Midwestern Jewish community is not characteristic of Jews who reside in metropolitan areas where life is organized around the voluntary pursuit of common interests.[4] The Jews of North City live in a more highly structured and clearly delineated community than do the majority of American Jews, whose social identity is less likely to rest on formal affiliation.

In the cities with the greatest number of Jews, there is no single Jewish community, but a variety of class and status groupings that do not demand special institutional participation as proof of ethnic birth. Born and bred in a world that appears to be populated entirely by chosen people, the Jews of New York, Philadelphia, Chicago, and Boston have little cause to be aware of their minority-group membership; they can afford to take their identity for granted. These Jews do not have to hedge their commitment around with a battery of clubs and organizations; their number alone safeguards their survival against the threat of the recalcitrant Jew. At the other end of the communal spectrum, there is the small town in which there are few Jewish institutions inviting affiliation.

4. See Max Weber, *The City*, translated by Don Martindale and Gertrud Neuwirth, for an incisive analysis of the principles underlying the social organization of the modern city (Glencoe, Ill., Free Press, 1958).

Thus, the Jewish community of North City, although typical of other American Jewish communities in many ways, demands a more active commitment of its members. Still, the conflict between community and career, however striking for the young Jews of North City, is by no means unique to them; it has been brought to the fore by pervasive changes in the larger society. The growth of large-scale organizations has demanded increasing involvement of their personnel and threatened the persistence of traditional local communities. The community is changing from a geographic area where one lives out the human comedy from cradle to grave to a status group whose special entrance requirements lead to a shared style of life. The community of yesterday is now only a temporary stop in the career of the organization man.

The impact of these structural changes has penetrated to the core of traditional Jewish patterns of self-employment rooted in particular ethnic communities. Jewish businessmen characteristically depend on the patronage of the in-group and the immediate availability of next of kin to carry on the family enterprise. Community organizers have in turn exploited their captive audience for community building to enhance their own status. New patterns of mobility freeing young Jews from the social pressures of the local community are all but subversive to the established structure.

Jewish communities, however, have never been founded on proximity alone. The common religious, national, and cultural backgrounds of their members have imposed stronger bonds. But the securely American status of the third generation and its increasing mobility have released it from old ties and community sentiments. Searching for new social anchorage, young Jews frequently turn to religion as the source of their identity. Although their "non-Jewish" social behavior belies their religious intent, they choose to be Jews. As other ethnic factors fail to provide satisfactory grounds for social identity, religion increases in significance—and utility. But finding religious roots in a nomadic existence without community support and institutional means of passing on the cultural heritage requires a new kind of social imagination. Is it possible to be a free-floating secular Jew without formal Jewish affiliations?

There are those who claim that neither alternative, institutional commitment or independent secular identity, is adequate. They relentlessly confront themselves with an ultimate choice between relinquishing their Jewish identity entirely or reaffirming their theological convictions. They do not find the adapted ritual of the modern synagogue sufficient grounds for religious identification. The emphasis of thoughtful young Jews is shifting from ceremony to belief, the one thing about Judaism that has resisted total acculturation and remains unique.[5]

Still, the third generation has yet to explain why it chooses to retain its traditional religious identity in the face of available alternatives. The ancient heritage of the chosen people may be a comforting source of roots to the new wandering Jew plagued by a twentieth-century anxiety about the nature of his identity. He shares with other Americans of all creeds a search for meaning, a renewal of the spirit. As Judaism takes its place among the other major American denominations, it becomes as acceptable as it is available to the younger generation. And it once more becomes a source of roots, this time for a new kind of nomadism, a new type of wandering Jew.

The ideology of the third generation is thus religiously rather than socially defined. The intellectual avant-garde of this most non-Jewish of all generations reintroduces theology into what has become a comfortable social habit.

5. See Arthur Cohen, "Why I Choose to be a Jew," *Harper's*, April 1959, pp. 61–6, for a discussion of the kind of traditional Hebrew theology being reconsidered today by a few young Jews.

But the yearning for an identity that does not identify invidiously remains unfulfilled, awaiting fruition in the generations to come. The claim to a dream is the American birthright, and the translation of dream into reality the drama of the changing generations.

Bibliography

I. BOOKS AND MONOGRAPHS

Anderson, Elin. *We Americans: A Study of Cleavage in an American City*. Cambridge, Mass., Harvard University Press, 1937.

Benedict, Ruth. *Patterns of Culture*. New York, Mentor Books, 1950.

Child, Irvin L. *Italian or American? The Second Generation in Conflict*. New Haven, Yale University Press, 1943.

Cohen, Elliot. *Commentary on the American Scene*. New York, Alfred A. Knopf, Inc., 1953. See particularly: David Riesman, "Introduction"; Morris Freedman, "The Jewish College Student: New Model," pp. 281–300; Herbert Gans, "Park Forest: Birth of a Jewish Community," pp. 205–22.

Cohen, Lillian. *Statistical Methods for Social Scientists*. New York, Prentice-Hall, Inc., 1954.

Davie, Maurice. *World Immigration*. New York, Macmillan Co., 1936.

Doby, John, et al. *An Introduction to Social Research*. Harrisburg, Pa., Stackpole Co., 1954.

Eisenstadt, S. N. *From Generation to Generation: Age Groups and Social Structure*. Glencoe, Ill., Free Press, 1956.

Fuchs, Lawrence. *The Political Behavior of American Jews*. Glencoe, Ill., Free Press, 1956.

216

Gerth, Hans and Mills, C. W. *Character and Social Structure*. New York, Harcourt, Brace and Co., 1953.

Glazer, Nathan. *American Judaism*. Chicago, University of Chicago Press, 1957.

Goldberg, Nathan. *Occupational Patterns of American Jewry*. New York, Jewish Theological Seminary Press, 1945.

Gordon, Albert I. *Jews in Transition*. Minneapolis, University of Minnesota Press, 1949.

Gouldner, Alvin. *Studies in Leadership*. New York, Harper and Bros., 1950.

Graeber, Isacque and Britt, Stuart, eds. *Jews in a Gentile World*. New York, Macmillan Co., 1942.

Handlin, Oscar. *The Uprooted*. Boston, Little, Brown and Co., 1951.

Heberle, Rudolf. *Social Movements*. New York, Appleton-Century-Crofts, Inc., 1951.

Herberg, Will. *Protestant-Catholic-Jew: An Essay in American Religious Sociology*. New York, Doubleday and Co., Inc., 1956.

Hughes, Everett and Hughes, Helen. *Where Peoples Meet*. Glencoe, Ill., Free Press, 1949.

Hutchinson, E. P. *Immigrants and Their Children, 1850–1950*. Census Monograph Series. New York, John Wiley and Sons, Inc., 1956.

Learsi, Rufus. *The Jews in America: A History*. Cleveland, World Publishing Co., 1954.

MacIver, Robert M. *Report on the Jewish Community Relations Agencies*. New York, National Community Relations Advisory Council, 1951.

Mannheim, Karl. *Essays on the Sociology of Knowledge*. Paul Kecskemeti, trans. London, Routledge and Kegan Paul, 1952. See particularly: "The Problem of Generations," pp. 276–322.

McWilliams, Carey. *A Mask For Privilege*. Boston, Little Brown and Co., 1948.

Pope, Liston. *Millhands and Preachers*. New Haven, Yale University Press, 1945.

Rose, Arnold, ed. *Race Prejudice and Discrimination: Readings in Intergroup Relations in the United States*. New York, Alfred A. Knopf, Inc., 1951. See particularly: Oscar and Mary Handlin, "Origins of Anti-Semitism in the United States," pp. 27–38; William Kephart, "What is Known About the Occupations of Jews," pp. 131–46; Meyer Greenberg, "The Jewish Student at Yale: His Attitudes Toward Judaism," pp. 309–21; Kurt Lewin, "Self Hatred Among Jews," pp. 321–32; E. Franklin Frazier, "The Negro's Vested Interest in Segregation," pp. 333–7.

Schermerhorn, R. A. *These Our People: Minorities in American Culture*. Boston, D. C. Heath and Co., 1949.

Seeley, John, R. Alexander Sim, Elizabeth Loosley. *Crestwood Heights: A Study of the Culture of Suburban Life*. New York, Basic Books, Inc., 1956.

Simmel, Georg. *Conflict and the Web of Group Affiliations*. Kurt Wolff and Reinhard Bendix, trans. Glencoe, Ill., Free Press, 1958.

——. *The Sociology of Georg Simmel*. Kurt Wolff, trans. Glencoe, Ill., Free Press, 1950.

Sklare, Marshall. *The Jews: Social Patterns of an American Group*. Glencoe, Ill., Free Press, 1958.

——. *Conservative Judaism: An American Religious Movement*. Glencoe, Ill., Free Press, 1955.

—— and Vosk, Marc. *The Riverton Study: How Jews Look at Themselves and Their Neighbors*. New York, American Jewish Committee Publication, 1957.

Smith, William C. *Americans in the Making: The Natural History of the Assimilation of Immigrants*. New York, Appleton-Century-Crofts, Inc., 1939.

Transactions of the Second World Congress of Sociology, 2. London, International Sociological Association, 1954.

Universal Jewish Encyclopedia. New York, Universal Jewish Encyclopedia, Inc., 1942.

Van Gennep, Arnold. *Manuel de Folklore Française Contemporaine*. Paris, Editions Auguste Picard, 1943.

Warner, W. Lloyd. *The Living and the Dead*. New Haven, Yale University Press, 1959.

Warner, W. Lloyd and Srole, Leo. *The Social Systems of American Ethnic Groups*. New Haven, Yale University Press, 1945.

Weber, Max. *From Max Weber: Essays in Sociology*. Hans Gerth and C. W. Mills, trans. New York, Oxford University Press, 1946.

Whyte, William. *The Organization Man*. New York, Simon and Schuster, Inc., 1956.

Williams, Robin. *American Society*. New York, Alfred A. Knopf, Inc., 1955.

Wirth, Louis. *The Ghetto*. Chicago, University of Chicago Press, Phoenix Books, 1956.

Wouk, Herman. *Marjorie Morningstar*. Garden City, N.Y., Doubleday and Co., 1955.

II. ARTICLES AND ESSAYS

Bierstedt, Robert, "The Sociology of Majorities," *American Sociological Review*, *13* (1948), 700–10.

Bressler, Marvin, "Family Patterns in Thomas' Study of the Bintl Brief," *American Sociological Review*, *17* (1952), 563–71.

Brogan, D. W., "Unnoticed Changes in America," *Harper's Magazine*, February 1957, 27–34.

Broom, Leonard, "Characteristics of 1107 Petitioners for Change of Names," *American Sociological Review, 20* (1955), 33–42.

Cohen, Arthur, "Why I Choose to be a Jew," *Harper's Magazine*, April 1959, 61–6.

Dean, John P., "Patterns of Socialization and Association Between Jews and Non-Jews," *Jewish Social Studies, 17* (1955), 247–68.

Fava, Sylvia, "Suburbanism as a Way of Life," *American Sociological Review, 21* (1956), 34–7.

Gans, Herbert, "American Jewry: Present and Future," *Commentary, 21* (1956), 422–30.

———, "The Future of American Jewry: Part II," *Commentary, 21* (1956), 555–63.

———, "Progress of a Suburban Jewish Community," *Commentary, 23* (1957), 113–22.

Gersh, Harry, "The New Suburbanites of the '50's," *Commentary, 17* (1954), 209–21.

Glazer, Nathan, "The Jewish Revival in America, I and II," *Commentary, 20* (1955), 493–9; *21* (1956), 17–31.

———, "Social Characteristics of American Jews, 1654–1954," *American Jewish Yearbook, 56* (Philadelphia, Jewish Publication Society of America, 1955), 3–43.

———, "What Sociology Knows About American Jews," *Commentary, 19* (1955), 275–84.

Goode, William, "Community Within a Community: The Professions," *American Sociological Review, 22* (1957), 194–200.

Goodman, Walter, "Bicker at Princeton," *Commentary, 25* (1958), 406–15.

Gordon, Milton, "Social Structure and Goals in Group Relations," Berger, Morroe et al., eds., *Freedom and Control in Modern Society* (Princeton, N.J., D. Van Nostrand Co., Inc., 1954), pp. 141–57.

Hicks, Granville, "Literary Horizons," *Saturday Review*, May 17, 1958, 16.

Hollingshead, August B., "Trends in Social Stratification," *American Sociological Review, 17* (1952), 679–86.

Kaganoff, Ben zion, "Jewish First Names Through the Ages," *Commentary, 20* (1955), 249–59.

Komarovsky, Mirra, "The Voluntary Associations of Urban Dwellers," *American Sociological Review, 11* (1946), 686–98.

Kugelmass, J. Alvin, "Name Changing and What it Gets You," *Commentary, 18* (1954), 105–14.

Lewin, Kurt, "Psycho-Sociological Problems of a Minority Group," *Character and Personality, 3* (1935), 175–87.

Minnis, Mhyra, "Cleavages in Women's Organizations," *American Sociological Review, 18* (1953), 47–53.

Park, Robert, "The Bases of Race Prejudice," *Annals, 140* (1928), 11–20.

Reissman, Leonard, "Class, Leisure, and Social Participation," *American Sociological Review, 19* (1954), 76–84.

Ribalow, Harold, "From 'Hungry Hearts' to 'Marjorie Morningstar,' The Progress of an American Minority Told in Fiction," *Saturday Review*, September 14, 1957, 46–8.

Riesman, David, "The Sociology of Jewishness," *Public Opinion Quarterly, 6* (1942), 41–56.

Roucek, Joseph, "Minority-Majority Group Relations in Their Power Aspects," *Phylon, 17* (1956), 24–30.

Seidler, Murray and Ravitz, Mel Jerome, "A Jewish Peer Group," *American Journal of Sociology, 41* (1955), 11–5.

Strodtbeck, Fred, Margaret McDonald, and Bernard Rosen, "Evaluation of Occupations: A Reflection of Jewish

and Italian Mobility Differences," *American Sociological Review*, 22 (1957), 546–53.

Tumin, Melvin, "Some Unapplauded Consequences of Social Mobility in a Mass Society," *Social Forces*, 36
(1957), 32–7.

Updike, John, "And Whose Little Generation Are You?
Or, Astrology Refined," *New Yorker*, October 5,
1957, 33–9.

Wirth, Louis, "The Problem of Minority Groups," Ralph
Linton, ed., *The Science of Man in the World Crisis*.
New York, Columbia University Press, 1944, pp. 315–
51.

Young, Pauline, "The Reorganization of Jewish Family
Life in America," *Social Forces, 12* (1928), 238–44.

Index

Acculturation: of minority groups, 5, 32; of first generation, 7–8; of second generation, 10, 19, 47, 82; of third generation, 17, 214

Age: of second generation, 63 n.; of third generation, 128, 199

Anti-Semitism: decline of, 136, 143, 147; North City experiences, of first generation, 47, 53, of second generation, 43–4, 63, 96, 108–9, of third generation, 44, 140, 146–7, 179–80; social consequences in North City, 56–7

Arts, patronage of: in second generation, 91; in third generation, 188–9, 199

Aspirations, changing: of first generation, 6, 18; of second generation, 8–9, 84, 123, 141; of third generation, 18, 139–45

Assimilation, attitudes toward, 190

Associations. *See* Clubniks; Lodgniks; Social clubs and organizations

Baltzell, E. Digby, 42
Bar Mitzvah, 166

Brogan, Denis W., 142

Business: family-owned Jewish, 67–9, 130, 133–5, 200; salaried employment in, 134–7, 147

Change, social, 21–3, 26, 123, 205–6

Cheder, 137

Children: education of, 83–4 (*see also* Education: religious); occupational choice, 85; social activities, of second generation's, 83, of third generation's, 170

Christmas observance, 92–4

Class. *See* Social class

Clubniks: attitudes toward lodgniks, 118; children, 73, 83–5; friendship patterns, 104–10; income, 66; intermarriage, 82; neighborhood residence, 74, 108–10; occupations, 66, 106; organizational memberships, 74, 94–6, 108; religion, 76–83; style of life, 73–4, 89–92

Community, minority: 3, 19, 21, 28–9, 74, 119–20, 206, 213; attitudes toward, in second generation, 12–13, 206–7, in third generation, 184–7; structure in second generation, 10–14, 101, 212–13; organizers

223

Success, 141–3, 206. *See also* Status: criteria of
Sunday School attendance of children: of clubniks and lodgniks, 83; of third generation, 153, 161, 163
Symphony Ball, 54
Synagogue: attendance, of second generation, 81, 151, 154, 157, of third generation, 151–7, 203; branches, 13, 76–9; Conservative, 42; emergence of, 12, 46; membership in, of clubniks and lodgniks, 79–80, of third generation, 155–6; Orthodox, 39, 45, 51, 154; reasons for affiliation, of second generation, 81, of third generation, 152–4; Reform, 42, 45; attitudes toward, 156; membership in, 65, 77–80; relationship to social class, 45

Talmud Torah: attendance of children, of clubniks and lodgniks, 83, of third generation, 161; enrollment, 51; role in community, 45–6
Third generation. *See* Generation: third
Tumin, Melvin, 31

Values: access to, 3, 5, 12, 19–20, 28, 123; competing systems, 4, 22, 30–1; differences in, between first and second generation, 8–9, between second and third generation, 19–20, 141–3; Jewish, of first generation, 8, of second generation, 119, of third generation, 209; non-Jewish, of second generation, 116–18, of third generation, 209; relationship to social class, 75–6, 112–13, 196
Verein, 39, 47

Wirth, Louis, 6
Wives: second generation, 19; third generation, 19, 170, 178, 187

Yichus, 13, 38
Yiddish, use of: in first generation, 39; second generation, 166, 196; third generation, 166

Zionism: attitudes toward, of second generation, 98, of third generation, 183; variations in ideology, 47

DATE	
DEC 17 1982	DEC 8 '71
GAYLORD	